The Startup Garden

How Growing a Business Grows You

The Startup Garden

How Growing a Business Grows You

Tom Ehrenfeld

McGraw-Hill
New York   Chicago   San Francisco   Lisbon
London   Madrid   Mexico City   Milan   New Delhi
San Juan   Seoul   Singapore   Sydney   Toronto

McGraw-Hill

A Division of The McGraw·Hill Companies

1 2 3 4 5 6 7 8 9 0   DOC/DOC   0 9 8 7 6 5 4 3 2 1

ISBN 0-07-136824-8

This book was set in Times New Roman by MacAllister Publishing Services, LLC.

Printed and bound by R. R. Donnelley & Sons Company.

McGraw-Hill books are available at special quantity discounts to use as premiums and sales promotions, or for use in corporate training programs. For more information, please write to the Director of Special Sales, Professional Publishing, McGraw-Hill, Two Penn Plaza, New York, NY 10121-2298. Or contact your local bookstore.

 This book is printed on recycled, acid-free paper containing a minimum of 50% recycled, de-inked fiber.

To my girls: Hetchen, Lucy, and Hayley

Contents

Foreword

Many of us become entrepreneurs because we're constitutionally unemployable. A job is nice, but we have an inner itch to do something we are truly passionate about—a need to build something we can shape in our own image, something that reflects not just what we do but also who we *are*. I've always viewed entrepreneurship not as a business concept, but as a *personal* concept. Entrepreneurship at its best is about creating a path that is uniquely suited to you as an individual and building a vehicle for driving down that path.

Consider the story of Yvon Chouinard, one of my favorite entrepreneurs. Chouinard began his business in 1957 as an 18-year-old kid who wanted nothing more than to pursue his passion for rock climbing. He borrowed $800 from his parents to buy a used anvil and forge to create new equipment for his first ascents of the sheer walls in Yosemite Valley. With no thought at all of building a big company, Yvon banged and clanged away on his anvil until he'd created a whole new set of pitons—metal spikes hammered into cracks of a rock to secure the climber to the rock.

One of Yvon's designs, the "Lost Arrow" (named after the famous spire in Yosemite) quickly caught on with other climbers and became a standard item for big-wall ascents. Climbers everywhere wanted Yvon's pitons, and so he began selling them out of the trunk of his car and backpack, wherever he happened to be climbing. Later, he formalized his business with a single mimeographed sheet that listed pitons and prices. This first "catalogue" told customers not to expect fast delivery during the summer months, as Yvon would likely be hanging in a hammock on the side of a sheer rock face, 2,000 feet above the floor of Yosemite Valley.

Yvon's business grew slowly, as he brought in enough cash to fund his rock climbing and to pay for making more pitons. Year after year, he gained more customers, and he made more pitons, and got more customers, and made more pitons, and so forth. He built momentum step by step, never allowing the business to *become* his life, but always keeping it as the vehicle *for* his life.

In the 1960s and 1970s, he added some key people to his operation. One was Tom Frost—another climber—who worked with Yvon to systematically redesign virtually every piece of rock-climbing hardware, from harnesses to piton hammers. The other was Kristine McDivitt, who assumed operating responsibility for the little company. The operation began to build more and more momentum—a million in revenues, then two, three, five, 10 million . . . All the while, Chouinard climbed at least six months a year, and other team members kept an active schedule of climbing, hiking, skiing, surfing—all in the name of "product testing," as they would say.

Then Chouinard's company made two pivotal breakthroughs. The first was a decision to marry the company to his passion for the environment. Recognizing that pitons left permanent scars in the rock, he reinvented the entire line of climbing gear—replacing pitons with metal nuts that slotted in the crack and could be removed without the use of a hammer. The second was to launch a line of outdoor clothing for serious adventurers, under the name "Patagonia."

And now you probably know the rest of the story. Chouinard gear and Patagonia clothing became the premium brands and the company took off. It was a classic "20-year overnight success story." What was once a business out of Yvon's rucksack became hundreds of millions in revenue out of an office complex in Ventura, California.

Yet even still, Choinard and other key Patagonia people retained their primary passion for the outdoors. Today, Patagonia stands as one of the most environmentally progressive companies in the world. It even pioneered the use of recycled plastic bottles into super-high-tech fabric for Patagonia jackets. And Yvon Chouinard, now in his 60s, surfs or climbs every week, close to home or in some adventurous location halfway around the world.

I share the story of Yvon Chouinard because he is a perfect example of what Tom Ehrenfeld is writing about in this book. I am excited that Tom has finally come forth with this work as a very practical guide to help those who would like to run their own operation not just as a business, but as a vehicle for their lives.

I don't know how many times I've been asked by friends, acquaintances, friends of friends, and acquaintances of acquaintances "I'm thinking of starting a business. Is there a book you would recommend to help me get going?" I'd usually give a list of books and tell them to read selected chapters from each one. Now, finally, I have the one book I'd like them to read as a starting point.

One of the most significant changes in the last 20 years is the transformation of entrepreneurship from a mysterious alchemy somehow practiced by superhuman visionaries into a practical discipline that nearly all people can learn. What was missing, however, was a practical synthesis that put all the key pieces in one place. In this book, Tom has synthesized the disciplines into a useful guide. But he has done it with a very nice twist. This book is not for those who want to start the next Cisco Systems or Apple Computer— creating *Fortune* 500 companies from scratch and becoming celebrity billionaires. This book is for the rest of us. It is for those who simply want to create a vehicle for their own lives and that reflects their own personal passions.

I have very few items on the bookshelves at my research laboratory—a few favorite books, a personal photo of my grandfather and my father on the day my grandfather died in a test-piloting accident, and a Lost Arrow piton, hand-forged by Yvon Chouinard on his original anvil. I keep it there as a symbol of the best model of entrepreneurship I know. As one of my great teachers, Rochelle Meyers, once told me, "The point of it all is to figure out how to make your own life a creative work of art that no one else could have painted." Entrepreneurship is about throwing out the paint-by-numbers kit approach to life and starting with a blank canvas. It's a more ambiguous path, but it is the only way to create a masterpiece.

And that is precisely what Tom Ehrenfeld is writing about in this book.

Jim Collins
Boulder, Colorado
August 23, 2001

Acknowledgments

So many people have helped me with this project that it's impossible to name them all. This project was conceived because of a friendly request from Eric Tyson. In Mary Baechler, I certainly found a business person whose experience convinced me of the tone of this book. Her love for her work has never overwhelmed her "self" in the business.

To all my cronies from Inc. Magazine, I thank you from the bottom of my heart. Inc. is and always has been a special publication that cares about the soul of a small business, and I've treasured my time there. Special thanks to John Case, Martha Mangelsdorf, David Whitford, Jerry Useem, Josh Macht, Josh Hyatt, Kelly Finnerty, Dave Freedman, Chris Cagggiano, Alessandra Bianchi, Ed Welles, Karen Carney, Nancy Lyons, and George Gendron.

Thanks to all who've helped me learn to write. From David Wiegand, David Rosenbaum, Art Kleiner, Tom Teal, Bill Taylor to Valerie Monroe—you are all finicky editors and that's a good thing.

Many people helped me by simply creating space for me to write. Thanks to Tom Fernandes for literally creating the space, as in building my office. Sal Clericuzio, thanks for providing a lifeline from the outside world. Larry Coe, thank you for helping me learn about financial literacy.

So many key readers along the path have offered support and encouragement: Campbell Ellsworth, Sarah Lawson, Cathy Olofson, Evan Grossman, John Maki, Sanj Kharbanda, and Todd Barrett.

Those along the way who have taught me about business include: Win Farrell, Bill Isaacs, Jack Covert, Avin Domnitz, Peter Senge, Jeanie Duck, and Amar Bhide

I've had the best set of business instructors one could ever ask for. I thank all the business people who went out of their way to spend precious time with me. For all your patience and time, thanks to Gus Rancatore, Scott Shaw, Amy Miller, Roxanne Coady, Marion McGovern, Kevin Cashman, Laura Peck Fennema, Martin Babinec, Catherine Fischer, Gregg Latterman, Ann Handley, Tom First, Tom Scott, and Gary Hirshberg.

Thanks also to those assistants, partners, and other folks who might not otherwise be mentioned, who make our work possible: M.J. Viederman, Christine Smith, Lori Perlstadt, and many more.

Over the years I've been privileged to work with many sharp editors and I'd like to thank the following people for helping me along my learning path: Pat Sullivan, Suzan Revah, Catherine Laidlaw, Mickey Butts, Luke Mitchell, Mitchell Hartman, Martha Little, and Stephanie Zacharek. Laureen Rowland, your support as a friend and supremely insightful reader is always dear to me. Jeanne Glasser, thanks for all you've taught me about business books.

Thanks especially to Jim Collins for all his advice. And Pete Duda, let me just say this—everyone needs a best friend in life. Kathy Fratus, thank you for freeing me up to write, for helping tend to the important things while I worked, and for all your support

Karen Budd, thanks so much for your invaluable research. To my friend Ellen Lamb, who parachuted in at the end of this project to provide research and feedback that proved key to my finishing this book, thanks so much.

To Daniel Greenberg, my trusted and inspired agent, thank you for seeing the promise of this book and for pushing me to make it right. Mary Glenn, my patient and brilliant editor, thanks for taking a chance on me.

Finally, thanks to my family. Liz, Mom, Dad, and Ruth, thank you for the love and support that has always nourished me. Ginger, thanks for the loving company you provide during the long hours of work. To my girls, Lucy and Hayley, thanks for the utter joy you bring to my life. And, Hetchen, thank you. Thanks for supporting and believing in me; thanks for sharing this journey. There's nobody I'd rather take it with.

Introduction

HOW DOES YOUR GARDEN GROW?

I owe this book to my friend Gus. Gus Rancatore is the founder, owner, and operator of Toscanini's Ice Cream & Coffee, three stores in my hometown of Cambridge, Massachusetts, that produce what is in my biased opinion the best ice cream in the world.

Gus is easy to spot. Most hours of the day or night you can find him behind the counter of his Main Street store, located across the street from a fire station and a couple of blocks from the campus of the Massachusetts Institute of Technology (MIT). He's the large, affable, slightly distracted fellow who's juggling three things as we speak, whether preparing an egg cream for a customer, checking the ingredients in the new batch of mango sorbet, or bantering with the supplier delivering coffee beans. Within his element of the store, Gus is the center of the universe. He's as comfortable talking politics with the local cops as he is managing his employees, many of whom are MIT students (some of them literally go on to become rocket scientists). At Toscanini's, Gus is the happy genius propelling the enterprise forward.

There's a spirit to the stores and the company that extends beyond Gus, and this force has always fascinated me. Like every small business, Toscanini's has a heart and soul beyond its owner's individual personality, and I've found over the years that Gus has learned as much from Toscanini's as he has put into the operation. It is this link that has led me to write this book.

I met Gus while I was a local reporter for the *Cambridge Chronicle* more than 15 years ago. Since then I have focused my work on the world of business, particularly small business. I chose to cover business for a simple reason. In Cambridge, I grew tired of reporting about what other people had to say, or what they thought, and I became much more passionate about what people did—the choices they made, the actions they took, and the consequences of those actions. The two best areas where these narratives take shape are crime and business. I chose to cover business.

As I learned more about business, particularly as a writer and editor at *Inc. Magazine*, it became clear to me that the line between the founder of a small business and his or her enterprise is a thin if nonexistent one, and that this blurring of life and commerce is what makes them exciting. Startups are as different and exciting as individual people. Many large companies are dynamic and fascinating, and the employees have great stories to tell—yet discovering the excitement often requires a journey through the heart of darkness. For me, the world of startups and the folks who launch them have always held the most allure. For at this stage, the passions, quirks and dreams of the founder or team mesh with the narrative of their company to create individual stories of growth beyond imagination.

That's why I have chosen *The Startup Garden* as the title of this book. Not to imply that you should go out and found a seed-and-soil company, as some have suggested. But simply to highlight the critical and living link between the growth of your company and your own personal growth. I have learned that growing a company grows you as an individual, and that this vital link between the person and the business nourishes the whole enterprise. This book attempts to articulate how. Wherever you are in the process of starting a company, I can help you take the next steps and gain more mastery in the process. *The Startup Garden* is designed to help you learn the skills necessary to be in control of your enterprise. Let's explore how.

HOW TO USE THIS BOOK

This book contains seven chapters. Each one identifies a particular skill that growing a business necessarily teaches you. First, you identify what you are good at, what you care about, and what opportunities are available to you. Then you learn to match these qualities with the specific needs of others. From there you develop financial literacy that grows your particular enterprise. You then learn to bootstrap, to manage others with clarity, and to implement a managerial system so that your business can (in theory) run without you. Finally, you learn to use your business as a resource for your continued growth.

Let me draw from the garden metaphor: Chapter 1, "Finding Your Calling," teaches you to identify the seed you want to grow; Chapter 2, "Planning as Learning, Learning as Doing," helps determine whether it is fecund. Chapter 3, "The Numbers that Count," plots *how* it will grow, and Chapter 4, "Bootstrapping," prepares you to nourish and feed the plant as it grows. Chapter 5, "Walking the Line," examines the human resources you'll need as your venture sprouts, and Chapter 6, "Just Managing," identifies how you make the transition from simply tending a plant to becoming a gardener. Chapter 7, "Perpetual Learning," teaches you how to step back and let your plant tell you what it needs—to understand what to prune, what to leave alone, and what to break off and plant as a new entity.

The Startup Garden begins, and ends, with chapters that explore how you learn and grow as you grow your business. The first chapter describes simple steps that you can take to identify who you are, what you care about, and what you are good at. It then proposes how to analyze your available resources and opportunities, and how you can use these energies as an engine to fuel your nascent venture. The final chapter examines how you learn with more mastery as your business begins to operate at a more powerful level.

The book's chapters are linked to one another naturally and necessarily. If you attempted to learn each of these practices in isolation, you might find them particularly insurmountable. Yet in the course of building a business, you will find yourself with no choice but to reach a point of mastery in each of these areas. By learning financial literacy, for example, or learning to set real boundaries in your relationships with employees, you will develop a toolbox of skills that enables you to grow your business in a meaningful way. You will learn these skills most powerfully when you do so from your own personal standpoint—that is, when you understand them in terms of your own needs, desires, existing skills, and capacities.

There is no one right way to start a company. Successful ventures are as varied as individual people. Yet learning the skills in this book gives you more choices and more control over the fate of your company. You can approach this daunting process with a greater sense of expectation and creativity, and a better idea of the choices you have available to you. There will always be elements beyond your control with a business: acts of God, stubborn customers, natural catastrophes, the impunity of Alan Greenspan. I can't promise smooth sailing. Yet by mastering these disciplines, you will be better prepared to address challenges and design the path of your success.

I have tried to distinguish *The Startup Garden* from the bulk of guides to entrepreneurs in one aspect above all. Although others provide lists and recipes that all startups must follow, I believe the key dynamic in every business is the individual or team that founds the company. All businesses may play by similar rules, yet they are run by individuals, each with his or her own set of strengths and passions and their corresponding closets of liabilities. To ignore this reality is to invite failure.

This book attempts to put all that necessary information within a personal framework—to help you learn such essential data as how to conduct market research, how to keep the books, or how to even come up with the right idea for a business *from your own perspective*. As companies grow and adopt policies and procedures, they do become like one another. But small companies, like Tolstoy's unhappy families, are different from one another in their own way.

This book recognizes and celebrates that difference.

Although no one right way exists for starting and growing a business, doing business requires that you play by the *rules*. From customers to employees, bankers to vendors, the various players in this game operate by a set of written and unwritten agreements. You must know these to participate. Moreover, *principles* exist for helping you navigate these rules. By learning a core set of principles and practices, I believe that all individuals can get in the game. I can't guarantee that everyone will achieve riches beyond their wildest dreams but I can promise that mastering these areas of practice will endow you with more control, and choice, in your enterprise—and by extension, in your life.

Although many successful businesses start with a great idea, they become healthy, sustainable ventures only after the founder or president masters sufficient skills to operate and renew the business beyond one specific product or service. You must master the skills that are discussed in this book in order to be in control of your business. I can't say how you will reach your destination nor can I guarantee that you'll get there. But, hopefully, this book will help you navigate the way.

Becoming an entrepreneur involves a shift in one's thinking. Working a job often means producing, being efficient, getting things done, accomplishing things. Acting entrepreneurially means creating value where it didn't exist before. It means seeing opportunity and taking the necessary actions to create value as a result. Deliberate steps and actions can help make this happen. Although the process may be intuitive to some, it can be learned by all, with the right approach. This book attempts to help people master this process.

I believe that in today's economy the heart of success—and your most important source of competitive advantage—is how well you know yourself, and how well that understanding animates the mission of your business. The degree to which you distinguish yourself by manifesting yourself in your business will determine your venture's success.

Here's one key thought driving this whole book. *Your business is the vehicle through which you realize your passion.* I choose each of these words carefully. *Vehicle*, to imply that the enterprise exists to take you and your stakeholders to a destination. No successful company is an end in itself. As we will discuss later, your business has a mission and a purpose, and the profit your business makes is a dependent variable tied to how well it consistently achieves what it sets out to accomplish. *Realize*, not just as in to realize a profit, but in the sense of the entire process of bringing forth an idea into the world as a finished product. And *passion*? Well, any successful entrepreneur will experience passion from joy and delight to rage and despair during the life cycle of a business.

The fact that you are reading this book shows that you have started your business. You are thinking about a product or service that will satisfy your needs—and those of more than a handful of customers. Now we will move forward by mapping out how businesses —and their founders—grow.

There has been no greater time to launch a small business than in the past 20 years. Today anywhere from 7.5 million to nearly 25 million small businesses exist, depending on whose data you believe. (I'll count the SBA definition, derived from tax returns, estimating roughly 5.3 million businesses with employees in this country.)

Yet these numbers only tell part of the story. Not only are more people starting their own businesses, but the culture of entrepreneurship has become ever more embedded in our culture. Business school students now rank entrepreneurship among their top career choices, while the number of courses on the subject has exploded in the past decade. More capital, in the form of venture money, angel investors, and commercial loans, is available for startups. And more resources —including everything from magazines to books to Web sites to peer groups—are now available for people with a desire to start their own company.

These macro changes have changed the rules of the game for would-be entrepreneurs. On the one hand, it's never been easier for an individual to launch a business. Startups are more culturally accepted, and resources are increasingly available, while technology, such as the Internet, and software, such as Quicken, give individuals the ability to gather information and take control of functions (such as accounting) that large enterprises could handle more effectively just a decade ago.

Yet all these changes have had one ironic effect. Although it is easier than ever to launch a business, these same changes make it harder for individual startups to thrive. Big businesses can now use technology to target smaller niches, whether products or geographic areas. The growth of massive retailers has laid siege on traditional mom-and-pop stores. And the general skill set of entrepreneurs today, many of them trained in business school or tackling their own companies after years of big company experience, is forcing everyone to become more proficient in the rules of the game.

Several years ago *Inc.* editor George Gendron noted that it's becoming harder for small companies to thrive based on one single proprietary idea. Today all small companies must become professional sooner than ever. As he puts it, the age of entrepreneurial novelty has given way to entrepreneurial execution. That's the bad news. Now, here's the good news: <u>you can do it</u>. The same changes that are making it easier for big companies to act small are enabling small companies to play big. And those small companies that have mastered the skills necessary to compete with larger players can use their size, speed, and self-awareness to greater advantage.

Here are a few final thoughts. I don't promise to cover every last bit of data you will need to know. If you are looking for a compendium of tricks, tips, and info on every last detail of starting your business, then I can, and do, recommend several all-purpose guides in the "Resources" section at the end of each chapter. Details like what type of office equipment to buy or how to market to one particular client are important and, in fact, are often the most pressing items on entrepreneurs' to-do lists. Yet all these details only matter *in context*. They become powerful actions when performed for a greater purpose, within a mission. This book is meant to help you create that vehicle. Sometimes the simplest decisions are the hardest to make. That's what we're grappling with here.

I started writing *The Startup Garden* during the explosion of the Internet with its brief bubble of wealth that seemed to promise fortunes to anyone launching an Internet company. Yet this book isn't about hitting the jackpot of huge IPO riches, nor is it about building a high-growth, venture-backed, high-technology company. There's a fundamental distinction between companies that use the Web in the context of launching a viable business, and those technology-based, venture capital-backed vehicles that are great ideas for companies but may offer little in the way of real customers or actual products. This book is meant for the former.

The time when one great idea alone made for a great company is over. Now, even in the world of the Internet, all startups are being forced to focus on the enduring rules of business success. So, I will certainly talk about the impact of the Web, especially as it affects how startups leverage technology, communicate with customers, and conduct myriad relationships and manage information. But I think that competence on the Web, like any number of managerial necessities, is becoming just one of a number of skills that all entrepreneurs must master to be in control of their future.

The explosion of the Internet economy has left behind one great, and often overlooked, entrepreneurial legacy. Regardless of those companies that have tanked, or failed to live up to their promises, I believe that the excitement surrounding new businesses in the past five years has exposed more individuals to startups, and startup culture, than ever before. As a result, more people not only merely believe they can launch a business, but they are taking steps to do so. That's a good thing.

One final word. I have spent the past five years running my own one-man show as a writer and editor. I've learned how to practice many of the lessons that I preach in this book. Before that I spent more than a decade absorbing the lessons of entrepreneurs who have launched their own successful companies. Many of these masters have taught me much about startups, and to a large extent I am sharing their wisdom in this book.

Ultimately, however, I can't teach you how to grow your particular business. You are going to learn on your own. I can help you ask the right questions and find the right resources. But, the practice of running your business will teach you the most important lessons. To quote my friend Gus, "Running a business is an existential process —you learn what you need to know only by doing it." But don't trust me too much. Go out and do it.

Let's get started.

1

Finding Your Calling

One day you finally knew what you had to do, and began.
— Mary Oliver, *The Journey*

YOU LEARN TO RECOGNIZE, ARTICULATE, AND, CAPITALIZE ON YOUR PASSIONS AND STRENGTHS

When Tom Scott and Tom First launched Nantucket Allserve in 1988, they had no great plans to build a world-class beverage company that many people recognize today as Nantucket Nectars. The two had both recently graduated from nearby Brown University, and they just wanted to run their own business. This urge, of course, was synonymous with a desire to run their own lives. Tom First always considered himself a "staircase person." When confronted with the choice between an elevator and a staircase, "I will always take the stairs over the elevator," he says, "because the elevator will stop anywhere—and on the stairs I can control my own destiny."

And so the two formed the company to avoid having someone else tell them where to get off, as it were. In their early days they ran a boat business, hustling for any work they could find. They towed and fixed boats, hauled fish, and delivered everything from bread to newspapers to the fishermen in Nantucket Harbor. The two set up a shanty for fishermen to open their scallops; they helped people wrap their boats for the winter. Then, during a slow stretch in the winter of 1989, Tom First made a peach juice concoction at a dinner party that everybody liked. Right away the two said, "Let's sell this off the boat next summer. We'll call it Nantucket Nectars." From that spark they grew a company that today does more than $50 million in annual business, and is a model of spirited management.

Mary Baechler hadn't intended to build a $10 million company with more than 100 employees when she first started selling baby strollers. She just wanted to save a little time. In 1984 she and her husband Phil, new parents at the time, were having trouble finding time to jog. So Phil cobbled together a device that let him combine his daily run with time with their new child. When people began asking where they could buy one of these strollers, the two would build one in their garage and sell it to the customer. Thus, was born Baby Jogger, Inc. Today the Yakima, Washington, company has diversified into crib liners and other baby gear. Mary, who remains head of the company, has learned a great deal about business through a venture that in its early years was conducted at their kitchen table. Yet she credits the emergence of the thriving and complex enterprise to the simple impulse to combine her time for jogging and being with her children.

Finally, consider Amy Miller. While studying to become a doctor at Tufts University outside of Boston, Miller started scooping ice cream at a local ice cream store named Steve's. At the time the store enjoyed the celebrity of being an early boutique ice creamery, offering high-premium sweets in a funky setting that drew crowds that formed lines literally around the block. The more Miller scooped, the more she fell in love with the business, and the more she discovered that she'd rather spend time tending to individual stomachs than to curing colds. Over time Miller learned the ins and outs of the business and, in 1984, launched Amy's Ice Cream in Austin, Texas. Today the company has eleven stores and does more than $3.5 million in annual sales.

Three different successful businesses—three different paths to success. None of these successful company builders were seasoned or experienced when they launched their nascent ventures. In fact, none of them had any practical experience about running a company. Rather, they were fueled by a passion for what they produced, and by a restless urge to control their own destinies. Though each brought different strengths and knowledge to their enterprise, they all grew their company at a pace comparable to their own personal development of skills. For each of them, as it will be for you, the simple process of running their company taught them what they needed to know. You can learn all you like from courses and books, but the act of running your company will always be the greatest source of growth and learning for you. It's similar to the difference between reading about a foreign country through guidebooks and movies and actually traveling there. Proficiency comes through practice, and business will teach you what you need to know.

The experience of these three people, and of many more entre-preneurs, reveals a truism about business startups that flies in the face of most dreamy legends about perfect jobs and dream companies. Even though many small business owners report a sense of control and happiness with their companies, they aren't all working on fantasy businesses based on childhood dreams or abstract ideals. Many of them found the right business through the process of being in business. This is not to say that they aren't basing their businesses on something they care about deeply. The two Toms couldn't be more passionate about making juice; to hear them talk about a new design for a bottle is not unlike a Formula One race car driver praising his or her car. Although your passion for what you produce should be at the heart of your business, it might not be the sole factor in determining what kind of business you should start. There are other critical factors. Now is the time to look at what they might be.

This chapter will teach you to listen to your own dreams and passions, link them to skills you have, identify your resources and opportunities, set personal goals and a mission, and then determine the most likely business that arises from this gumbo.

"I think that opening a business is a leap of faith. You are abandoning a lot of your old life, you can't return to anything. And there is an unnerving aspect to it. Most small business owners think about that stuff, and forget about it. They aren't necessarily triumphing over their fears—they are just setting them aside."

—Gus Rancatore

"I think one of the things that has been a big learning experience has been to fess up to what your strengths and weaknesses are. That is a really hard thing to come to grips with. If you want your business to grow you have to really make sure that the people you are working with tell you what you are doing wrong. And you must be willing to listen. Otherwise you get stuck between wanting to grow your business and being willing to take the time to really address your shortcomings. And that is a big learning process. You can sort of fudge it in a big company, where somebody may pick up the slack for you. But in that large company you may not have enough leverage for that weakness to have consequences. In a small company it might mean everything."

—Roxanne Coady,
Owner of R. J. Julia Bookstore in Madison, Connecticut

OR . . . NOT?

Before you start borrowing money and building storefronts in the air, it's a good idea to be sure that you really want to embark on this journey. Before we analyze your individual venture, you must ask one fundamental question: Do you really want to start your own business? Launching a business is a massively time- and soul-consuming project with the potential to destroy your personal life, cripple your self-confidence, obliterate your personal (and family) resources, and pretty much leave you with nothing to show for it. It's wise to think long and hard about whether you really want to embark on this journey. See the sidebar "Should You Keep Your Day Job?"

Personally, I don't believe that there's one easy-to-define entrepreneurial type. Rather, anybody with commitment and the right mind

SHOULD YOU KEEP YOUR DAY JOB?

Tempting as it is to jump into your new business with both feet, it makes sense for most people to hang on to their day jobs, at least for a while. Your new venture may very well be an extension of your activities at your current job. Maintaining continuity helps in several ways.

First and foremost is simple cash flow. Your business may not be profitable enough to pay you a salary for some time, and the longer you can keep regular income flowing in, the more time and energy you will be able to dedicate to refining your product and developing loyal customers.

Along with a salary, of course, are benefits—which should never be taken for granted. Health insurance is a major expense, assuming you can even qualify for the same level of coverage you have. If you have a chronic health condition, such as high blood pressure or diabetes, you may have trouble finding coverage at all. Moreover, having your company withhold taxes and pay half your social security is a blessing. Startup entrepreneurs are often shocked by their first year of taxes as a separate enterprise; having extra taxes withheld from your salary can soften the blow.

Finally, existing businesses often root you in the industry you want to be in, and keep you connected with potential customers, partners, and other supporters. For many small-business owners, especially in service sectors, their employer may be their first and most important client, or may even be an initial source of capital. The right day job can be an apprenticeship as valuable as a graduate degree. While you're working, you may also be able to take advantage of job-related training programs that will help you later on: professional continuing education, computer training, human resources workshops, and more.

continues

SHOULD YOU KEEP YOUR DAY JOB? (*continued*)

There's no reason you can't start a company while holding on to a job. Yet if you choose to do so, you need to be honest with your employer about your plans. "You have to have an agreement with your present employer because starting a business is time-consuming," says Ann Marie Stanton, who was able to start her own business as a Los Angeles-based antique jewelry dealer while working as an assistant to HMS, an established dealer. Stanton kept close ties with her former employer after branching out on her own. "It was important not to burn any bridges," she said, "and Harriet [her former employer] is a big supporter of mine."

set can master the skills and take the actions that make one an entrepreneur. As leading business thinker Peter Drucker puts it, "Everyone who can face up to decision making can learn to be an entrepreneur and to behave entrepreneurially. Entrepreneurship, then, is a behavior rather than a personality trait."

This is not to say that starting a company is for everybody. There are many considerations to take into account when considering whether to launch a business at all. First, you should match up whether you are at some fundamental level a good fit with starting a company. Try looking back over your life, for example, and asking whether you have acted entrepreneurially before—in anything from finding or creating a market for funky earrings to creating something you wanted but couldn't find elsewhere. For a quick check on how you might be tested with your endeavor, see the sidebar "Who Wants to Be an Entrepreneur?"

Launching a business is not as risky as you might imagine. There's a huge distinction between *risk*, which can be characterized

WHO WANTS TO BE AN ENTREPRENEUR?

Here is a set of questions that will test your entrepreneurial mettle. Don't worry about being graded on your responses. I don't believe that this comes down to a pass-fail distinction. But these questions are designed to help you examine whether you will find the entrepreneurial life to be a good fit with your disposition:

- Can you afford the time, energy, and consuming distraction?
- Are you comfortable making decisions?
- Do you learn new skills quickly?
- Are you willing to admit, and compensate for, your weaknesses?
- Does selling come naturally to you?
- Have you ever started a business before?
- Can you live with rejection and loneliness?
- Do you have personal and emotional support for the enterprise?
- Do you mind giving orders?
- Are you willing to brave uncertainty?
- Do you believe, truly believe, in what you are about to do?
- Are you prepared for your life to change completely?
- *And*, if you answered no to every question on this list, are you still willing to start? Today?

as the possibility of loss, and *uncertainty*, which refers to the lack of knowing what lies in your short- and near-term future. In many ways, launching a business is less risky than sticking it out at an uncertain job in today's fast economy. Just look at the continued layoffs from established companies, which even in the best of times are striving for ways to streamline staff in the name of efficiency.

Moreover, startups are more resilient than most people think. Research done by economists at the *Small Business Administration* (SBA) shows that more than half of all businesses last for more than two years, while another half of that number lasts for four years. The actual stories behind these statistics reveal a healthier scenario than these numbers indicate. These statistics include the large number of businesses that are sold, or whose owners retire, or close shop for greater opportunities. Granted, certain industries are more failure prone than others, but don't forget: You aren't starting a statistical probability. You're starting your own unique business.

As opposed to risk, startups do introduce a highly revved-up *uncertainty* to your life. You will have to learn to get better at answering questions and get better at figuring out what the salient questions in your business life are. You'll have no guarantee of steady income, professional validation, or the simple psychic comfort that comes with having an established job. You may not know where your next round of capital will come from, or how you will produce the next generation of your product, or whom you will be working with tomorrow, or next month. You may just not know how you'll solve some pressing problems—life will come to resemble my favorite exchange from *Shakespeare in Love*, where Henslowe assures Fennyman that, "Strangely enough it all turns out well." When asked how, he replies, "I don't know. It's a mystery."

Just remember that you will be making a conscious decision to integrate your personal and work life with your company. This decision brings both pros and cons. On the plus side, you have more control over your own destiny—and realize a more immediate link between your behavior and the success of your business. You enjoy greater ownership, both literal and psychological, over your work. You increase your opportunity for wealth. You have the chance to truly design the job you want, and to create a product or service you deeply believe in. You pursue knowledge and increase your expertise on an ongoing basis. You satisfy people.

Of course most of these conditions bring with them a dark side. Owning the company, for example, often results in just the opposite —feeling completely possessed in life by a time- and energy-sucking enterprise that leaves you with no other life whatsoever. Moreover, launching a company often deprives you of all those lovely perks and benefits that are second nature to established companies. (Are you prepared to fix your copier when it breaks down and do your own FICA paperwork?) Starting a company means abandoning all the fixed structures and the order they bring into your life. Finally, start-ing a company can be an invitation to loneliness—not merely because you give up the water cooler and other huddles of friendly support, but because you will be constantly asking strangers to validate your endeavor, and only sometimes succeeding.

For these reasons, and many others, launching a business just isn't right for everybody. There's nothing dishonorable about work-ing for others, nor is there any shame in honestly assessing the toll that running a business takes—and deciding against it. Consider the choices made by Jim Collins. This former Stanford Business School professor had the opportunity to build a lucrative consulting company based on the success of his book, *Built to Last*. After the book's 1994 publication, Collins could have earned significant money consulting, training, and going on the lecture tour. Yet he chose to follow the pre-cepts he laid out in his book. So, he defined his own mission and values, and chose his life accordingly. This meant being an educator above all else, which forced him to make a few key decisions.

First off, Collins decided not to hire anybody full-time. "If you start hiring people full-time and building a firm, you build in fixed overhead, which means that you'll have to sell something to support it," he says. Collins couldn't do this and remain aligned with his personal goals. "I don't sell and I have no interest in selling," he says. Although he does see some clients and gives an occasional lecture, he has set ground rules for himself. He limits all clients to a maximum of three days per year. He limits his consulting or teaching activities to less than 25 percent of his time, and he devotes at least 50 percent of his time to the creative work that is at the heart of his books. The tradeoffs for him have been to forgo greater financial gain for a better realization of what he values most. "If I were to start a Built to Last consulting company, I would have made 5 to 20 times what I made over the past 5 years," he said recently. "Instead, I am my own self-endowed chair."

Collins understands that building a business calls for a massive commitment in terms of time, resources, and attention. Don't kid yourself—starting a business is a huge leap, and it's critical that you be clear about the demands that starting a business imposes on your life and on those around you.

WHAT IS A BUSINESS?

Let's start by defining just what a business is and does.

There are several ways to think about a business. You could define a business as the various activities and processes that you conduct in order to produce a bottom-line profit. This definition is

"Business will occupy an enormous amount of your living, breathing hours. I don't really know much about working for someone else's company, but I know that I bring my work home with me every day of my life. It has its benefits and its problems. I suppose that employees can put it behind them when they walk out of the door. But as an entrepreneur you need to carry the little picture in your mind all of the time, but still be able to step back and look at the forest."

—Tom First, Nantucket Nectars

perfectly acceptable for an accountant or a professor. Yet the point of this book is to help you see an equally valid definition of a business that tilts this equation. You should also consider a business to be all those financial considerations that enable you to produce something you care about. Is your business the first, or second, type of entity?

This, of course, is a trick question. You must think about your business as both.

At its very core, a business is an organized entity that provides goods or services to customers in exchange for money, or some other form of currency. Ideally, eventually, and finally, consistently, it does so for a profit. That's because businesses *add value*, through sweat or smarts, or processes, or scarcity, in ways that customers can't or won't do on their own.

The range of value-adding activities is vast. You might apply your sweat and muscles to turn a pile of bricks into a sidewalk, or a mass of construction materials into a new room. You might use your thinking hat to ease someone else's technical confusion. You might have a knack for turning scraps of cloth into clothing or quilts. You could be a natural matchmaker between companies and executives seeking jobs. The possibilities are as unlimited as the number of stars in the sky.

Regardless of how you add value, the word *exchange* forms a critical part of this definition. Businesses always exist in relationship to a web of customers, employees, partners, vendors, and other community members. Businesses by definition exchange and relate to a wide skein of people and organizations. We'll explore the notion of customers, selling, and meeting needs throughout this book. It is critical that you understand the importance of your business as an entity that conducts social intercourse with other people and organizations. At this very early stage in your business, even though you are determining what it is you have to sell, be sure to hone your listening skills. One identifiable trait of most superb entrepreneurs is their ability to read other people.

As you begin to conceive of your own individual business, it's important to think through how you will add value for your customers. Every business structure and type carries advantages and disadvantages. Companies with low barriers to entry (meaning that they are very easy to start), for example, are often great starter companies for beginners. Endeavors like cleaning houses, swapping collectibles, or consulting on something you know about all require few resources beyond what you have. This means you can get started easily and hopefully hustle your way to success. This inviting opening has definite drawbacks. First, anyone else can enter the field as easily as you did, giving you a run for the money. Second, you are probably relying more on your individual hustle than on the creation of something that is uniquely yours. Although you can earn more simply by working more, your profits are ultimately related to, and limited by, your personal hours.

You can also pursue a venture that adds value at a much higher level than a simple lifestyle type of business. Yet this too has its pros and cons. There are pie-eyed entrepreneurs who have sought to build new satellite systems, creating new communications networks. Great idea, and, should the venture work, it would be very, very hard to knock off by others, but of course one needs vast financial and organizational resources to make such a plan pay off.

WHAT DO YOU WANT FROM YOUR BUSINESS?

Figuring out what you want from your business requires you to answer one simple question first: What do you want out of life?

Sure, this question may seem a bit daunting. Although it's very helpful if you can come up with your mission in life, going through this exercise can sometimes become grueling and distracting. So, for the sake of starting a business, let's define this question in some specific ways. You should know enough about what you want to achieve in life to be able to make some important decisions concerning your business goals. In particular, you need to consider what you want, and need, your business to achieve for you.

There are several fundamental areas to consider. The first, for lack of a better word, is *lifestyle*. What kind of life do you want your business to accomplish for you? What type of people would you like to spend your time with? How much personal time do you need? Where do you want to live? What types of conversations do you want to have every day? What kind of objects do you want to handle, to learn more about?

Your particular business must match up to your own personal goals. Remember that dreaming of building the next Microsoft is not only unrealistic, but brings with it huge sacrifices. Many people want an enterprise that provides a living while keeping them hooked into something they care about deeply. "We didn't want to set up a business," says Tom First of their early days, "We wanted to set up a lifestyle—and the business came out of it. Initially the business was the vehicle for the lifestyle." At the outset, the two designed a simple enterprise that enabled them to live on the island, deal with folks they liked, and maintain a degree of control over their lives.

Your business ambitions should be aligned with your personal goals. Will you be happy to have a simple, profitable, though low-growth venture? If you dream about opening a bookstore, or making children's sweaters, can you live with just one location or a regional business? How close to the operations of your business do you want to be? (For example, do you want to be in the kitchen cooking the meals, or in the office running a string of restaurants?)

Also, you should consider your aspirations. In other words, what do you want your business to help you achieve? Do you really want to change an industry, change the world? Is it critical that you design a business that addresses a social issue, directly or indirectly, large or small? What effect would you like it to have in the world?

Then, of course, you should consider what this business should do in terms of your financial goals. Remember that in all likelihood your business probably will *not* make you super-wealthy. It will certainly not bring you immediate riches. The vast majority of entrepreneurs who leave steady jobs to launch companies take at least several years to earn their former salary; many don't ever match their former income. Yet the value of doing work they love, or the satisfaction of ownership, or the equity they build in their company, are often more than compensatory.

Of course, realizing your dreams certainly could lead to riches. I wish you well in that regard, but here's a simple point: Launching a business simply to become rich is almost certainly a path to failure. Shift the equation from simply trying to maximize dollars to <u>creating value</u>, and you will achieve financial success in the course of creating a good business. Most entrepreneurs who realize fortunes do so as a result of achieving a specific, and often nonfinancial, goal. I defy anyone to find a mission statement of Bill Gates that reads "to become the richest man in the world." No, his Croesus-like wealth came as a result of his realizing a far more ambitious plan: to put a personal computer on the desk of every person in the world.

Certainly, your company must generate enough income to support you and your family—if that is what you determine to be your goal. Perhaps you have a spouse or partner to handle that end, or maybe you have something to fall back on. The trick is to weigh your financial goals against your personal goals, and then conceive of a business that addresses both. The answer to the financial question always boils down to a far more important question: What do you really want from your business?

I can't stress enough how important it is to be very clear about why you are launching this venture. For as you grow, you will always need to return to your simple goals as a compass.

WHAT'S YOUR BUSINESS?

Businesses, even small startups, come in many different shapes and sizes. How about yours? Let's try to think about what you would like to provide, and accomplish, with your business. Let's start by looking at the four key ingredients of *passions, skills, resources,* and *opportunities.* Again, remember that businesses are not some abstract idea, but a viable enterprise for which you will serve as the heart and soul. So, you must now begin to take stock of what is possible for you.

The four key areas for you to assess in deciding what type of venture is appropriate for you are passions, skills, resources, and opportunities. You need to assess each with an open mind, and then think through how they might translate into a business.

As you go through these exercises, be sure to ask your closest friends and family to keep you honest because you need others to keep track of where you have not been fully able to recognize hard truths. Unfortunately, a business will amplify your individual weaknesses, as your flaws will emerge miraculously as operational quirks and

---

"Successful entrepreneurs do not wait until the Muse kisses them and gives them a bright idea; they go to work. Altogether, they do not look for the biggie, the innovation that will revolutionize the industry, create a billion-dollar business, or make one rich overnight. Those entrepreneurs who start out with the idea that they will make it big—and in a hurry—can be guaranteed failure. They are almost bound to do the wrong things. An innovation that looks very big may turn out to be nothing but technical virtuosity, and innovations with modest intellectual pretensions, a McDonald's, for instance, may turn into gigantic, highly profitable businesses. The same applies to nonbusiness, public-service innovations.

Successful entrepreneurs, whatever their individual motivations—be it money, power, curiosity, or the desire for fame and recognition—try to create value and to make a contribution. Still, successful entrepreneurs aim high. They are not content simply to improve on what already exists, or to modify it. They try to create new and different values and new and different satisfactions, to convert a material into a resource, or to combine existing resources in a new and more productive configuration."

—Peter Drucker, *Innovation and Entrepreneurship*

liabilities. So, the best way to manage this element is to be open and out front with them from the beginning.

Of course, the first person to listen to when starting your business is yourself. Your business begins when you identify your strengths and passions and they manifest as a business or service. As entrepreneur and author Paul Hawken states, "Your business must be an extension of who you are and what you are trying to learn and achieve." So, ask yourself: What do you love? What are you good at? What change do you want to realize in the world? Let's look at how to take the first steps toward this goal.

Passions: Quite Simply, What Do You Care About?

What matters to you? What hobbies do you have? What do you want to change in the world? What do you enjoy doing? What do you go out of your way to learn about? What is important enough to interrupt your daily routine? What makes you cross the street? Look back over your life and identify the interests or callings you've pursued that have been meaningful to you. Think beyond simple hobbies or vocations and include personal themes or causes to which you've devoted your time and energy. Try answering this question without any con-

---

"Persistence, and the act of believing in yourself is the most powerful and underrated attribute needed for starting a business. When you start a company everyone else's mission will be to tell you you can't do it. Competitors will beat up on you, investors will try to reduce your worth to get a better deal, and on and on. You need to have a reason to believe in yourself."

—Gary Hirshberg, Stonyfield Farm

sideration whatsoever. Don't edit. Just write down five things that really matter to you. If you can't come up with five, that's okay; perhaps you are absolutely certain about your top two or three, but do be open-minded.

Remember that you will be spending countless days and hours on the guts of your business, so it's important to identify areas that compel you, offer opportunities for your own growth, and enable you to produce something that others will care about deeply.

Many great businesses arise from matters that the founders care passionately about. Founder and owner, Wayne Erbsen, of Native Ground Music grew a simple business from his passion for traditional American music. Originally a hobby of his, Erbsen launched a business gradually by recording and writing about music from the time of the Civil War and regions such as Appalachia. Working out of his home, Erbsen has produced CDs and books that form the basis of a

---

"I don't know how people design or plan every kind of business, but I usually think that any business starts with a product. It's hard to think of a business where you shouldn't build a great product before anything else. Entrepreneurs are cluttered with the concept that systems, business plans, margins, investors, advisors, press releases, etc. have something to do with starting a business up and running. BS. It's all about a product and telling your story to the customers. If the product is great, it's an easy story to tell. If the product sucks, it's a hard story to tell. Refine your product and design it in a way that it can be reasonably available to your target customers and you have a business. Eventually you have to figure out the economics. But if your product sucks and you have all the economics figured out, you will have wasted your time (and your investor's money)."

—Tom First, Nantucket Nectars

---

company that sells more than $200,000 worth of products a year. "I'm tied to my products," he says, "I've put my heart and soul into my product and it means so much more to me when someone calls me, I can say, 'I wrote the book and I sang the songs, how can I help you?'"

Or consider Laura Peck Fennema, who was making a great living as a stock analyst for Rothschild, Unterberg, and Towbin in the late 1980s. By day Fennema would pore over data and write reports on communication equipment; at night and on weekends she would turn to her passion for concocting aromatherapeutic products, such as facial cremes or bath remedies from natural botanical oils. Fennema would share these products with her mother and three sisters, who all encouraged her to find a broader audience.

And finally, in 1989, Fennema did. "I came upon a real defining moment: whether to spend my whole life focusing on how much money I could make, or how to spend it focusing on what I loved to do and had a real passion for," says Fennema. After a year of preparation, learning the market and testing the viability of a venture based on her passion, Fennema took the leap. She launched Essentiel (spelled to reflect the French origins of the word) Elements in 1989, and today the company has more than forty employees and did more than six million dollars in business last year.

Skills: What Are You Good At?

The categories are broad and range from technical chops in computer programming to a proficiency at writing zippy prose to more abstract personal skills such as being good at listening to people or understanding how to gather and make sense of information. Your skills comprise everything you have learned in school or in previous jobs, as well as any innate talents and abilities that you have. This exercise is most akin to analyzing what you offer prospective employees; yet now you are thinking about applying these talents to your own venture.

Don't focus simply on the most valuable skills you have, the ones that you believe will lead to the most money in the market. For now just write down everything that you believe you are good at. For Shari Fitzpatrick, her skill was making chocolate-dipped strawberries. That's right—chocolate-dipped strawberries. She was making a fine living as a mortgage broker in Sacramento, California, partly because she would pamper her realtors with baskets of chocolate-dipped strawberries. The gifts became so popular that Fitzpatrick eventually began selling them out of her home, and then opened a shop in 1991. Today her company has four stores and a booming Internet presence.

Resources. What resources are readily available to you? Cash? Tools? Expertise? Contacts? Property? Fame? In many ways the crucial link between an idea and its realization are the resources that make it happen. You may just be able to derive a meaningful business from the resources to which you already have access. "People tend to overestimate the importance of the resources that they have —and underestimate the importance of the ones they don't," says restaurateur and serial entrepreneur, Scott Shaw. In the next chapter we'll explore how to realistically assess the resources your venture will need, and how you will gain access to them. In the meantime, you should think about how your resources on hand might suggest a viable business.

Opportunities: Finally, Think About What You Could Do Immediately

Perhaps you could ply the trade you now practice within a large firm on your own. Maybe you could tweak it just a bit, and launch a company on that. Try to answer this question. Say you are reading this book on the weekend. What type of business could you begin operating this coming Monday?

Is there a product or service that you need but can't find somewhere, and is this something you know enough about to provide to others? That's what Ann Handley and Andy Bourland did when they launched a Web site named ClickZ in May of 1997. At the time, the two were just looking for a quick way to realize some extra cash. Bourland had been hit with an unexpected tax bill and needed supplemental income from his job as director of business development at the Internet company Andover.net. He and his friend Handley, a journalist who had written for trade publications, but lacked Web experience, realized that they were both frustrated with the lack of information available on how to market online. They couldn't find the type of site they wanted.

 So, they created their own. Handley and Bourland launched ClickZ as a Web site where people who worked on the Net could share their marketing expertise. Because Bourland was familiar with the technology, he could quickly learn enough Web-design skills to present a rudimentary site; Handley tapped her skills as a freelance journalist to produce copy. Before long they had formed a community of people who did business on the Web; by providing information from folks in the trenches, and providing a place where others could learn, the two had created a profitable company. The site grew slowly, but surely, earning them a profit from the early days, and in 2000 they sold the company.

FROM IDEA . . . TO COMPANY

Okay, now you must take these four areas and brainstorm how they might lead to a business. It's likely that you have already begun to focus on one product or service. Yet before settling, go beyond literal thinking—try lateral thinking as well. In other words, don't edit yourself. Just write down your ideas and possibilities without judging how good they are. You may surprise yourself with an opportunity you hadn't considered.

Finally, begin sifting through your prospects and decide on your first choice. Don't worry about whether this will be your absolutely final decision. Your business in all likelihood will evolve as you begin the process of testing its viability.

Congratulations, You're in Business

At this point you have defined your goals, and identified your skills, passions, resources, and opportunities. You have begun to match a type of business with your own goals and assets. You have acknowledged how much work lies ahead of you, and you have begun to think through the resources, in terms of cash and people and general wherewithal, that you will need in the months ahead. Now you should take the next steps. As you do, here are a few final thoughts.

Trust Your Heart

At this stage in your nascent venture, concentrate more on what you care about rather than simply what you are good at. Choose a path that is formed by your passions more than your skills. You can always learn new skills, but you won't stop caring deeply about the things that really matter to you. Finally, don't worry so much about the market for your product—yet. Start with what matters to you, and not whether somebody else will buy it. You are your first customer. If you are passionately convinced of your offering, you will be able to persuade customers (or investors or partners, for that matter) simply and naturally.

Start Talking

The strength of your business will be fundamentally tied to the strength of the networks that you form. Although you may not know everyone you need to get your business running, now is the time to begin to create formal and informal networks that support and nourish your venture. You begin these ties with a simple telephone call. Call 10 friends, 10 potential customers, 10 competitors, 10 vendors, and 10 potential investors. Ask them what they think of your venture. Ask them what they need for theirs. Ask them about what works for their company, and what has been their greatest failure. Ask why. Great entrepreneurs are naturally curious. They achieve breakthroughs and see things differently because they have more information at their disposal. Keep in mind that many successful people are willing to share what they know. So, if you respect their time by preparing for an interview and limiting the time, you will be surprised at the information you can glean from unlikely sources.

Get Started

According to research from Boston College Professor Paul Reynolds, it often takes a lot longer for individual businesses to become viable, profitable enterprises than many people imagine. Some businesses take as long as seven years—yes, seven years—before showing sufficient profits for the owners to support themselves from the enterprise. Naturally, your particular business probably won't take this long —but you should never assume that profits will come immediately. That's why it's important to get started now—to take those first steps toward putting your energies into a business context. You've begun to identify what you have to offer and merged that with a thought toward how it adds value.

Moreover, you won't necessarily end up where you start out. Professor Robert Ronstadt of Pepperdine University says the entrepreneurial process is guided by the corridor principle, by which the act of moving forward makes it possible for you to land in the right entrepreneurial place. "The learning process allows you to see opportunities you didn't see before," he says. So don't censor yourself. Already we've heard of businesses such as Nantucket Nectars that began simply as a vehicle for two young college grads to live the lifestyle they wanted. Yet many of today's largest corporations also started life as vehicles for their individual founders. Perhaps the most famous is Hewlett-Packard, which also grew out of the lifestyle choices of the two founders; the company produced a variety of different products before finding a successful and profitable market.

Congratulations. You've started your business. There are all kinds of indicators for when a business begins—when you give it a name, when you record the first sale, when you incorporate, or when you file a tax form. I believe that the fact that you have conceived of a business means that you are in business. Now let's move on to thinking about what makes your business unique and valuable.

"Prior success, confidence, and the ability to sell are all absolutely vital to becoming an entrepreneur, and can be cultivated. The things that have helped me are a track record of prior successes, a well-rounded skill set, and a knowledge of the market."

—Desh Deshpande, Sycamore Networks

TOOLS AND RESOURCES

Further Reading

Repacking Your Bags and *The Power of Purpose* were written by Richard J. Leider (Berrett Koehler, San Francisco, 1995 and 1997); although no book can fully illuminate your purpose in life, Leider does a lovely job of helping you think through your most important passions and motivations, and provides a set of exercises that links your passions and values to your calling. Although Lieder focuses his exercises on jobs and careers, his fundamental approach applies to starting a company as well.

Amar Bhide's essays appear in *Harvard Business Review on Entrepreneurship* (HBS Press, Boston, 1999). Bhide's essay "The Questions Every Entrepreneur Must Answer" is a classic in which Bhide proposes a simple structure asking you to assess your personal goals, your strategy for how well the business achieves these goals, and then runs through how well you are equipped to execute this strategy. Bhide reminds individuals that your business will require different strengths and skills from you as it grows, and illuminates how your role as the founder must evolve as the business grows.

Working Solo by Terri Lonier (John Wiley & Sons, New York, 1994). Although Lonier's books focus on the single business practitioner, the core value of her advice relates to most startups. Lonier provides innumerable tips on everything from how to set up an office to how to incorporate your business, and she sheds light on the mind-set you'll need to maintain and operate a business on your own.

Start Up by William J. Stolze (Career Press, Franklin Lakes, New Jersey, 1999) and *Beating the Odds in Small Business* by Tom Culley (Fireside, New York, 1996) are two books of wisdom on tactics from veterans who have founded their own successful startups. Each provides the helpful voice of experience steering you through some of the early events to be expected at this point in the game. Culley does a particularly good job of debunking myths about the startup process and rooting the enterprise in the nuts and bolts of running a business, rather than the grand ideas or abstract notions of what it takes.

Governmental Resources

Finally, a number of governmental and other organizations exist that provide terrific help for entrepreneurs in the form of resources, mentors, and information.

The federal government makes a great deal of effort to educate and help small business owners. Information and, in some cases, financial support are available not only from the Small Business Administration, but from government agencies as diverse as the Federal Reserve, the Department of Labor, and the Federal Trade Commission.

The comprehensive guide to government resources is *Crossing the Bridge to Self-Employment: A Federal Microenterprise Resource Guide*, published in May 2001 by the Federal Interagency Working

Group on Microenterprise Development. This group consists of representatives of 13 government agencies, including the Small Business Administration, the National Women's Business Council (**www.nwbc.gov**), the Federal Banking and Credit Union Regulators, the Federal Housing Finance Board, and the departments of the Treasury, Agriculture, Commerce, Labor, HUD, and Health and Human Services.

The *Small Business Administration* (SBA, **www.sba.gov**) is the government's central online resource for guidance on starting your business, loan programs, and other resources. The SBA has a terrific, expansive, inclusive site that answers questions, educates you on the theory and practice of small business details, lists local offices, and gives you information on virtually every federal program that might help you out. The site's Starting button lets you research local legal requirements, essentials of a business plan, tax issues, and more. Through the site, you can find a mentor or even find a business opportunity. Better yet, the site has links to all these resources.

The Financing button is your link to the SBA's 17 different loan programs, including specialized programs for microloans, loans to support pollution control, loans for veterans, and several programs to support community development enterprises. The link also takes you to information about accessing the secondary market and about Small Business Investment Corporations, which are government-sponsored enterprises that provide venture capital to entrepreneurs. The site also contains an excellent kit covering most of the logistics of getting started, at **http://www.sba.gov/starting/indexstartup.html**.

The *Service Corps of Retired Executives* (SCORE, **www.score. org**) matches up veteran executives with new business owners for counseling and mentoring. SCORE also offers guides on financing, setting up a home office, online purchasing, and many other topics. SCORE's online Business Resource Index provides links to dozens of sites to help you with everything from calculating a loan payment to recruiting employees to conducting in-depth market research.

The U.S. Chamber of Commerce (**www.uschamber.com**) and your local chamber of commerce can be good resources for networking and business development. Local chambers of commerce often have mentoring programs of their own, and may offer members deep discounts on everything from office supplies to liability insurance.

12/18/01 Develop Website
        Put Flipdolls on
Mission Statement
Invite Roben to next house party
Key phone #'s
Pink case for Roz

2

Planning as Learning,
Learning as Doing

I learn by going where I have to go.
—Theodore Roethke, "The Waking"

LEARN TO THINK PRAGMATICALLY ABOUT CUSTOMERS, MARKETS, AND RESOURCES

Entrepreneur Jerry Kaplan has founded two highly visible companies, with starkly contrasting results. In 1987 he formed Go Computing, to fulfill his own personal obsession of making handheld computing possible to a broad consumer audience. This idea appealed to Kaplan. It appealed to a handful of computer aficionados, and it appealed to venture capitalists. The problem was that it didn't appeal to customers. Well, not enough customers to support a company, that is. Nor, incidentally, was it doable. For while Kaplan was ultimately able to raise—and spend—$75 million, he and his expert colleagues failed to successfully develop handheld computers that were ready for broad adoption. Years later Kaplan contrasted his failure in this field with his second (successful) startup, an Internet auction company named Onsale (since merged with Egghead).

"In my first company I was trying to build an entire industry," he says, "whereas in my second my goals were a lot more manageable." Kaplan learned that ambition counts for a lot in launching a successful business, but that if your vision is too grand you will fail. The difference between the two ventures? While each was based on a passion of his, the second enterprise was far more viable, says Kaplan. He launched Onsale only after conducting focused research and planning. Kaplan spent an enormous amount of time talking with customers about whether they wanted what he was selling, and he proceeded only after he determined that he could actually deliver this product to a ready community of customers.

Likewise, as you begin the process of talking to people, conducting research, and putting together a business plan, you must ensure that what you offer meets the needs of a sufficient number of people to sustain a company. In other words, while the seed to grow your company may have been generated by listening to yourself, now you must learn to listen, to really listen, to others. Now is the time when you gather the necessary information to determine whether your idea will make a viable business. And you will spell out how you will make it happen. As you test the viability of this venture, you will learn to fuse the act of planning with the act of learning, and to further apply this learning by doing it within the context of taking incremental steps toward actually running your business. In other words, your planning process is both pure and applied research and development—a process by which you are starting to generate customers and cash.

In Chapter 1, "Finding Your Calling," you explored your skills and values, analyzed your available resources, and came up with an idea for your company. Now you need to figure out whether—and then how —you can produce and sell your product consistently and over time. You need to take a step back and assess what type of organization will enable you to deliver the goods. This chapter will help you think about your company in a structured and systematic way, and take the first steps toward actually operating the business. Moving from idea to reality means figuring out how you will find, reach, and satisfy your customers, how you will generate cash, and how you will build a company with the capabilities to fulfill—consistently—those first two goals.

At this point you should be thinking above all about three ideas that begin with C: *customers*, *cash*, and *company*. The first two are fairly self-evident: All businesses are fueled by the two resources of customers and cash. You add value by delivering a product or service to your customers, who in turn swap enough money with you for your enterprise to turn a profit. And so while the planning process repre-

---

"The best place to make decisions is from inside the war. When you are on the battlefield, you know the truth, you can feel the pressure, the pace, the strengths and weaknesses. You cannot feel these things from afar. You won't know the truth and you can't guess the right move. You must play the game to know how to play the game."

—Tom First

---

sents an abstract exercise in figuring out how this will happen, it can —and should—also serve as a hands-on discipline in which you start to generate both customers and cash. The act of being in business means turning a dispassionate eye toward analyzing how you will produce and serve these two forces in a consistent and disciplined manner. You are able to converse with customers and generate cash by building a company that delivers the goods. This chapter is about making all three C's a reality.

Start with *customers*. As you begin to merge the passion you have for what you want to do with the external world, you will begin to grapple with this fundamental force in a more systematic way. First and foremost, you will need to analyze them and their needs, and determine how you will deliver the highest value to them over time.

But there's more—you now have customers in the larger sense: employees who buy into your vision and sign on with the company and investors who pledge their support to the business. Regardless of whether your company needs millions of dollars in venture capital or a simple psychic boost from a few enthusiastic customers, you must now learn to connect with the people who fuel your enterprise.

This requires you to develop one more skill for your entrepreneurial toolkit: the ability to sell. This doesn't necessarily mean a huckster's craft for cold-calling clients and pushing arcane financial instruments on rubes. It means that you need to get comfortable at conveying your enthusiasm for your company to others, and learn how to ask others for support, without blushing. To some people this action comes as naturally as walking; to others it's an acquired skill. Whether naturally or not, however, at this point you will start selling your vision to customers, investors, employees, and supporters.

Next, there's the simple, though profoundly important, matter of *cash flow*. Not profit, which can be a theoretical construction of the balance sheet, or capital, which is another critical supply, which may have nothing to do with your current fiscal health. *Cash flow* is the measure of cash, actual cash, that is coursing through your business. Without cash your company will cease to exist, so you need to track the rate at which money is coming in and going out—at a profit. We'll go into this in greater detail in Chapter 3, "The Numbers That Count," which is devoted to tracking the key financial numbers that reveal the health of your enterprise. But for now, cash flow should still be a guiding force for your enterprise. Your business should be generating cash from your customers, and, even after accounting for startup costs, that money should exceed your expenses.

Finally, you will now need to create a *company* that delivers on the promise you've been dreaming of. Think of your company as the sum total of the resources, assets, processes, skills, people, and activities that enable you to add value by delivering goods and products to your customers. The company is the vehicle by which you deliver the goods. It's one thing to have a great idea for a product or service, however, the real challenge lies in taking the steps in the real world to make it so. Now you must begin to make explicit just how you will consistently and profitably do what you say you will. This is the fun stuff.

One quick note: As you begin this process, you may choose to buy a business rather than launch a new one of your own. (See the sidebar "Buying a Business.") Should you go this route, I believe that you must still go through the following planning process.

BUYING A BUSINESS

Buying a business is the fastest way to start one—but it comes with its own challenges and risks. When you are considering buying a company, be sure to assess how well this particular business fits into your personal goals and values. Are you buying a business for the income, the opportunity, the lifestyle? All the same criteria that apply in starting a business also hold for buying one.

The next most important question to ask is: *What* are you buying? Are you buying stock? Are you buying fixtures? Are you buying the business's name? Customer list? If you're buying the customer list, does the seller get to keep a copy as well, and will the seller continue to use that list to solicit business? Business machines or equipment? Supplies? Real estate? If it's a retail property on a lease, how will that lease be transferred to you? Do you get to keep the phone numbers? What about the Web site? Will the seller pay off all the business's debts before the sale is complete? (Believe it or not, it may make sense to assume some of the business's debts, if it's a business that needs revolving credit from suppliers.) Will the business's employees stay on after the sale? What contracts are in place and how will these transfer to you?

The process of evaluating a company in many ways represents a proxy for writing a business plan. That is, the process of determining the health of this particular company, and the context in which it operates, should teach you the essentials of what you need to know to operate this business. Of course, the process of buying a company can be complex, and you will probably need a lawyer to help you set a fair price and conduct the transaction. The best book on this topic is *A Basic Guide for*

continues

BUYING A BUSINESS (*continued*)

Valuing a Company by Wilbur Yegge. He walks you through the process of valuing—and buying—a company.

One last thing: Before you buy, list the additional investments you'll need to make. Add those costs to your purchase price, then estimate what your income will be over a given period of time. If you are financing the purchase, will that income be enough to service your debt, pay your employees, and support the ongoing costs of doing business?

Business Plans and Business Planning

As you begin to realize how to make your business come to life, always keep in mind that planning is doing. Entrepreneurs by definition act resourcefully with the materials and opportunities at hand. This approach characterizes the planning process as well. You can't afford the luxury of too much formal planning, especially if it isn't yielding immediate results. Yes, create a plan, and, yes, do formal planning—but always do so in the context of taking further steps toward refining your business concept, and getting it going.

In recent years the business of planning business plans has emerged as an enormous industry staffed with experts and consultants, fueled by books and software, and subsidized, by and large, by the sweat and sleeplessness of countless entrepreneurs. This industry has created a big danger for novices: They confuse the business plan with the business. Eager starters often sink so much time and passion into creating a formal plan that they convince themselves that success on paper translates into actual sales. Going down this path can lead you to become too committed to decisions that you feel you must make, simply because you have argued so often for them. Becoming too emotionally invested in a plan makes it easy to mistake the map for the territory—to allow the plan to distract from the actual business. This makes it hard to see that opportunity often lies on an adjacent path and requires open eyes to spot.

There's a world of difference between business plans and the formal process of planning for your business. Both are crucial for your enterprise. Yet, while there's overlap, one should neither neglect one area nor confuse the two. Your business plan is simply a document, a blueprint, a recipe for your company. So, while a great business plan can certainly lead to a great company, the most important reason to create a business plan is to begin the practice of planning and realizing your company.

"If you do a business plan as a way of thinking through every step that you need to think about, then it is going to be one of the best things you have done," says owner Roxanne Coady of the R. J. Julia Bookstore in Madison, Connecticut. Coady warns, however, that people should never forget that the plan exists to prepare for running the business. "If you do a business plan because it is what a bank or an investor wants to see then it is useless," she points out. "Preparing

---

"The greatest benefit of having a business plan is that by writing everything down, you are more likely to see the entire picture, and you are more likely not to forget some important steps to prepare yourself for this huge venture. Launching a business without a business plan is much like building a house without blueprints. You can certainly do it, but when you discover a mistake in the foundation after the roof is shingled, you're really going to kick yourself."

—Bernard Kamoroff, *Small Time Operator*, p.37

---

a plan for outsiders is a very different activity than trying things out and then putting your plan into action. You don't want the process to take over."

Prior to opening her bookstore in 1990, Coady spent a year conducting research on her prospective business. By day Coady worked as a partner at the Big Eight accounting firm BDO Seidman; at night, and during whatever time she could carve out, Coady prepared a voluminous plan that filled out a thick looseleaf notebook. She conducted market research, spoke with other bookstore owners, explored the numbers, and learned everything she could about bookselling. And from that process Coady created a business plan that detailed exactly the store she hoped to create. As a result of this extensive planning, Coady was able to launch her business with a clear idea of what the store would offer to customers, and how it would deliver on its promise. "The core ideas and objectives about my store haven't changed at all from that plan," Coady says today. Adding, "The numbers—like in most business plans—weren't right, but everything else was."

Business plans serve both internal and external roles. To distinguish between the two, I'll capitalize *Business Plans*, with a grain of salt, to refer to the external process, and keep the process of planning lowercase.

Externally, a good Business Plan becomes a calling card and a sales vehicle for your nascent venture. Many different players in the startup process may want to see your business plan for different reasons. Business Plans earn credibility with potential backers, not to mention employees, media, customers, and others. The document proves to potential backers and supporters the validity of your prospective business. The plan also shows how the money you are trying to raise will be spent to further your business's goals. Finally, it serves as a résumé for your business, introducing the idea and the viability to others.

Internally, business plans force you to develop an explicit awareness of how your business will take shape. Preparing a plan forces you to articulate not just what you want to do, but how you will do it. Writing a plan also helps you begin to take the actual steps you need to actually run your business, to serve as a practice run for running your company. The importance of this process can't be underestimated. The process keeps you honest by rooting you in the actual nuts and bolts of an industry rather than allowing you to build abstract arguments about why a company should succeed. Customers don't buy arguments or ideas. They turn over their cash for real products and services.

Your planning comprises the conscious action of getting relevant information for your business and adding value by using this data or insight to create a unique product or service for customers. It's the deliberate, systematic, step-by-step process by which you take your grand idea of a business and turn it into a living, breathing, operating business. This entails everything from gathering data about your market or your competitors to having lengthy talks with customers

---

"There are a few times when you need a business plan. When your banker wants one, for example, or when an investor is sizing up your company. But a good plan will help you get a loan about as much as a nice suit will. Like a classic business suit, a good business plan helps you fit in and puts people at ease. It's like camouflage. It will not get you the loan or the investor's money if you otherwise lack the assets to guarantee the loan."

—Mary Baechler, "Do Business Plans Matter?"

---

about their real needs. Smart entrepreneurs use the planning process as practice for running the business—for taking the baby steps that give you the know-how and confidence to run your own venture.

You don't have to give up your day job to begin gathering information and developing relationships with customers. In 1990 Marion McGovern tested the viability of her prospective company M Squared by sending out 1,000 questionnaires to potential clients while she was working as a consultant for Booz-Allen. McGovern planned to open a new type of employment agency, one that would provide interim expertise to startups in the form of highly skilled executives in such fields as accounting, marketing, human resources, and manufacturing. McGovern jokes that the responses were a "resounding maybe." She couldn't conclude with any certainty that she could build a business in this market. Yet, by the same token, McGovern also learned enough to believe there was no reason her business *couldn't* make it.

McGovern's research nonetheless provided two crucial boosts to her company. First of all, simply taking the steps toward launching a company helped her locate a partner. While conducting a focus group among prospective clients, McGovern was intrigued by a woman who said she wanted to launch a company with other women. Her goals, in fact, matched up so well with McGovern's that she ended up taking her on as cofounder of the company. You will find

---

"A lot of people spend too much time trying to set a company up and not enough time *being* a company. By the time people have built the company and found the building and given out options and gone through all these other exercises they have no company left. People should just do it."

—Gregg Latterman, Aware Records

that the process of gathering information will also turn up resources that will nourish your venture (see the sidebar "Are Incubators Appropriate?").

ARE INCUBATORS APPROPRIATE?

Recently there was a brief public infatuation with incubators as vehicles for helping entrepreneurs jump-start their companies. In short, incubators are organizations that provide resources such as office space, capital, and other shared infrastructure, in order to accelerate the startup process for people who believe they need this additional help. There are many compelling reasons for fledgling entrepreneurs to hook up with incubators. Office space, technical support, capital; what's not to love? Yet the tradeoffs are often onerous. Some incubators ask for a hefty piece of the company. And there's the deeper issue of control, and the fact that you may lose control of the company. And all for the *promise* of rapid development of your idea.

Yes, you may rev up your startup through an incubator, but here's a critical principle to keep in mind: Wisdom doesn't scale. You can't learn faster just because you have lots of resources. While it's important to move fast, to strike when opportunity presents itself, and so forth, your company often needs to determine its own rate of growth. And it sometimes needs to discover its own market and focus without the pressure of outside experts.

That's not to say incubators can't work. Incubators can work when you are comfortable with the tradeoffs involved, and when you hook up with a center that has experience at mentoring new entrepreneurs. A great resource on incubators is the National Business Incubation Association, which can be reached at 1-740-593-4331, or on the Web at **www.nbia.org**.

And second, by testing out clients, by using the research process as a way of lining up future customers and refining the service her company eventually provided, McGovern minimized her risk and exposure, and gained a high degree of confidence when she opened shop.

So, What's Your Plan?

Now, having spent some time beating up on business plans, let's examine the formal requirements of a plan, while keeping in mind the broader role that preparing this document plays in helping you become pragmatic about realizing your idea. The following areas depict the important questions that your business plan must help you to answer.

So, let's define a business plan. A *business plan* is a formal document that describes what your business does, says who you and your partners are, elaborates how your business will make money, and shows just why your business has a chance of succeeding. It's one part résumé for your company, one part business card, and one part blueprint for the venture you'll build. And, just like a personal résumé can generate excruciating agony in answering simple questions, so can a business plan make you sweat. (See the sidebar "The Business Plan Outline.")

Here are the fundamental questions your plan must address:

- What do you offer?
- Who are your customers?
- What opportunity are you responding to?
- Who are your competitors?
- What resources do you have?

- Who are the people behind your company?
- How will you execute your plan?
- How will you make money?

Let's examine each of these areas in more depth. As we do, keep in mind that you should add "consistently, over time" to each of these questions. In other words, as you answer these questions in the near term, always be aware that you will need to constantly revisit them, adapting and evolving to provide different answers as your business gets off the ground. Finally, remember always that the end goal of exploring these questions is not to produce a business plan. The result of your going through the process of answering these questions is to get your business going.

WHAT ARE YOU SELLING?

So you've come up with the idea for your company. Now you should take some time to define exactly what it is you offer. Are your goods high-end, high-quality, high-priced, or do you see them as affordable products for a broader audience? In what context will people use them? Are they high or low quality? Above all, what *distinguishes* your product?

Chances are you've founded a company based on a product or service. Your "music" could range from a particular style of food in a restaurant to a new design in children's sweaters to a high-tech invention that enables people to access their email differently. Gus Rancatore of Toscanini's, for example, wanted to produce a more distinctive ice cream than existed at the time. "I wanted different flavors than was out there. And maybe because I had spent time at a lot of

THE BUSINESS PLAN OUTLINE

In a nutshell, here are the formal elements of a business plan. Bankers and other players who may lend you money or other forms of support will expect you to follow this basic outline. For more details, see either the Tiffany-Peterson or Pinson-Jinnett book.

The *Executive Summary* captures the essence of your business very simply, in one or two pages. Distill what you offer, to whom, what characterizes your business, and what distinguishes it in the field. State what is unique and special about your company.

The *Company Description* provides more nuts-and-bolts information about the business: where you are located, what you provide, and other organizational details. It also details the logistics of your company. How, in particular, will you produce and sell your product? The *Market Description* details the opportunity that your company is responding to. Competition, customers, and other related factors go here.

The *Management* section shows the qualifications of you and your team. It lists you and your partners, your board members if you have any, and other players who are supporting the venture.

The *Financial Documents* attest to the financial health of your venture. If you are already up and running, you will provide current and historical income statements and balance sheets. For your planned company you will provide financial projections. In any case, the purpose of the financial statements is to prove that your business makes money—and, if you are applying for a loan, that you have the means to repay it.

"The first time that we wrote a business plan, it was written by Tommy and me—alone. The second time we wrote a business plan, we did it with a woman who worked for our investor. She talked us into writing a plan that worked on paper, but made no real life sense. When you build a plan for your business, you need to know in your gut that you can hit your goals. The best thing to remember is that the little pit in your stomach that says 'I hope we hit these numbers' is telling you that you won't. Overpromising and underdelivering on anything sucks. You will hate the process, your investors will lose confidence in you, and you will spend more time explaining why you missed the numbers of your plan than you will building your business. Work very hard to write a plan that you know you can hit and then sell that plan to your board and your investors . . ."

"The plan should support the efforts to build a great product—not to appease your investors. Your primary job is to sell a plan that strengthens your product to people that simply want to make money—this is all about salesmanship, not finance."

—Tom First, Nantucket Nectars

schools, my interest was a bit more academic. I wanted to find flavors from other ethnic groups—whether Chinese or Mexican or Indian." Today some of his most popular flavors, such as Mango Sorbet, or Khulfee (a mix of Indian spices), are influenced by other cultures.

Or, your music could simply be filling a need that isn't being met. Gregg Latterman formed Aware Records in 1993 with the goal of finding and signing unknown musical bands. Yet he was competing with the major record labels. So, Latterman chose to release compilations rather than entire albums, a move that helped him break out up to a dozen bands rather than just one; and he formed a highly productive and frugal company to find the bands and get the word out.

Your company could also be based on a service—such as your consulting skills in a technical area, or your ability to organize people's closets. Many computer technicians, for example, who have learned to fix other people's equipment have gone on to launch consulting businesses in this field in the past decade.

Or, your company may also be based on *process* excellence—that is, you believe you can do specific tasks better or faster or cheaper (or all of the above) than others. Such a road invariably demands a lot of sweat and hustle—but if you can establish your methods and get them to the point where you can offer this service to a multitude of customers, and even sell your expertise to others, then you will have created a high source of value. Regardless of its physical or intangible qualities, work hard to think through the compelling and unique attributes of your company's offering.

You need to define how your product or service is distinctive from what already exists. One critical tool that consultants and business school students toss around is the notion of competitive advantage, which means, pretty much, what the words suggest. What edge does your company have in the marketplace? What do you offer that others don't, and, more importantly, how do you plan to maintain that edge when others discover the great thing you've produced and want a piece of that action? (See the sidebar "Competitive Advantage".)

Here's a helpful question to get a head start on that problem: What unique conversation can you have with your customer? What unique experience are you creating? Think about the Grateful Dead's music. Former lead guitarist Jerry Garcia used to say, "Our aim is not just to play better than other bands or to play different music than other bands. Our goal is to play the music that only we can play." If you can come up with the qualities or features that are distinctively

COMPETITIVE ADVANTAGE

HBS Professor Michael Porter has become rich and famous for popularizing a laborious model of what distinguishes and differentiates businesses in the marketplace. The fact is, he's onto something that even startups should consider—the idea that they must offer something that others don't, or they must offer a product or service that other companies can't produce as well as they do. As you refine your own business idea, Porter's theory is eminently applicable. You should constantly ask yourself two questions. What can I produce that others are not producing right now? And then the key follow-up: How can I continue to produce this product or service better (faster, and cheaper too) than anybody else?

yours, then you are distinguishing yourself from others in the market. You're answering the key question of how you will fend off others who want your niche.

You should think about how your passion or vision may not revolve around a specific product but a new *experience*. That's how CEO Howard Schultz built Starbucks into a cultural force. Schultz was by no means the first to invent a fine cup of coffee, but he did pioneer the notion of serving upscale cappuccinos to the morning commuter. Schultz built a thriving company based on the simple idea of providing fine coffee to consumers in cozy, convenient cafes. In fact, Schultz's vision for Starbucks was based on applying the success of a different culture's tradition to the United States: His goal with the company was to recreate the social experience of Italian espresso bars by serving high-quality coffee drinks in comfortable neighborhood cafes.

On a more modest level, consider the Parkway Speakeasy Theater in Oakland, California. Owner Catherine Fischer started this combination pizza joint-movie theater in 1998 with a singular vision. "I wanted to be able to go see a movie, and while doing it get a pizza and a beer. That didn't seem too much to ask," she says, adding, "I hated having to spend $10 for a ticket, be forced to buy green hot dogs and nasty popcorn, and being asked if I wanted to supersize my drinks." So she and her partner conceived a movie theater that would serve fresh pizza, offer beer, and give patrons sofas and a place to put their food while they watched the movies. They were able to raise $150,000 from a friend, and with that money renovated an old theater in Oakland. Since then it has built a loyal community following and has earned national recognition for some of its clever promotions.

WHAT ARE YOU *REALLY* SELLING?

Try this useful exercise. Set aside for a moment the literal guts of what you plan to offer, and think about the need or solution that you are meeting for the customer. Work backward from their perspective. In the process you can cite both the literal product you are delivering and the underlying service it embodies. In the short term this may force you to rethink your basic product, and in the long term may lead you to expand in ways you hadn't imagined. (See the sidebar "What Is Your Company's Reason for Being?")

The best example of this might be IBM, which founder Tom Watson grew by always positioning the company as a *solutions* provider. Salesmen (no slight intended) were taught to learn the needs of the customer and to sell a product that helped rather than simply try to bully the most expensive product on them. Developing an innate

WHAT IS YOUR COMPANY'S REASON FOR BEING?

The following statements of core purpose come from the book *Built to Last* by Jim Collins and Jerry Porras:

- 3M: To solve unsolved problems innovatively
- Hewlett-Packard: To make technical contributions for the advancement and welfare of humanity
- Merck: To preserve and improve human life
- Nike: To experience the emotion of competition, winning, and crushing the competitors
- Wal-Mart: To give ordinary folk the chance to buy the same things as rich people
- Walt Disney: To make people happy

ear for the market enabled Watson to discover a far larger market for his machines than he had originally invented. The company, incidentally, was initially named CTR, or Computing-Tabulating-Recording Company, and sold time clocks, scales, and tabulating machines. When Watson initially began selling computers, for example, the target was scientific institutions and not businesses. But when companies began to buy the machines for bookkeeping purposes, IBM switched gears and served that market—thus handily beating Univac, which had pioneered the computer long before but failed to understand the needs of its customers. In other words, IBM served its customers rather than trying to reform them.

WHO ARE YOUR CUSTOMERS?

Assume that you have a passion for your company's product or service. The key to converting this into a business is connecting this with customers. Over time you need to do so on a more structured and formal basis. This requires a more formal analysis of who your customers are and how they will behave.

As you speak with people who are buying your product, or who represent potential buyers, start to identify them in detail and assess their behavior toward your company. You need information that enables you to figure out what your relationship will be over time—how intimate you will be with your customers, how you will solve their problems, how often you will deal with them, and so on. Who will purchase your product, and how much they will spend? Will they buy once, or many times? Will your customers be primarily first-time or repeat buyers? What will keep them loyal? How will you find ways to sell more goods to the same set of customers? You should work especially hard to determine why they will be spending their money *with you*. That is, what will be the compelling attraction of your company?

WHAT OPPORTUNITY ARE YOU RESPONDING TO?

Your company exists in many different contexts: social, technological, and economic. Can you identify the relevant external changes that add to the inevitability of your company's success? What makes it likely that your company can succeed today as opposed to last year or five years ago? For example, technological changes enabled a company like Palm to finally roll out a handheld computer. Societal changes enabled Starbucks to become such an explosive force. Cultural changes led to consumers being more open-minded to microbreweries. Answer the previous questions to help you analyze your current opportunity in more detail. (Also, see the sidebar "Peter Drucker's Dos and Don'ts of Successful Innovation.")

PETER DRUCKER'S DOS AND DON'TS OF SUCCESSFUL INNOVATION

Do:

1. Begin with a systematic analysis of the opportunity. Be sure to apply your innovation to the appropriate place. Don't look, for example, to demographic change as an opportunity for a new industrial process.

2. Look, ask, listen. Talk to customers. Don't just research markets and crunch numbers, but get a real sense of what people want by talking to them. "Successful innovators use both the right side and the left side of their brains."

3. "An innovation, to be effective, has to be simple and it has to be focused." Trying to do more than one clear thing will leave people confused. The greatest praise for the innovator, in fact, would be for people to say, "This is obvious. Why didn't I think of it?"

4. Effective innovations start small. Don't try to revolutionize an industry. Think about doing one specific thing. Staying small at the outset also makes it easier to change and adapt as needed.

5. Nonetheless, aim your innovation at leadership. "If an innovation does not aim at leadership from the beginning, it is unlikely to be innovative enough, and therefore unlikely to be capable of establishing itself."

Don't:

1. "The first is simply not to try to be clever. Innovations have to be handled by ordinary human beings, and if they are to attain any size and importance at all, by morons or near-morons. Incompetence,

continues

PETER DRUCKER'S DOS AND DON'TS OF SUCCESSFUL INNOVATION (*continued*)

after all, is the only thing in abundant and never-failing supply. Anything too clever, whether in design or execution, is almost bound to fail."

2. "Don't diversify, don't splinter, don't try to do too many things at once. This is, of course, the corollary to the "do": be focused! Innovations that stray from a core are likely to become diffuse. They remain ideas and not innovations . . ."

3. "Finally, don't try to innovate for the future. Innovate for the present!" Drucker points out that innovation requires neither technology nor knowledge, but, above all, market knowledge, which "supplies a better core of unity in any enterprise, whether business or public-service institution, than knowledge or technology do." He continues that, "unless there is an immediate application in the present, an innovation is like the drawings in Leonardo da Vinci's notebook—a "brilliant idea."

"And finally, innovation is an effect in economy and society, a change in the behavior of customers, of teachers, of farmers, of eye surgeons—of people in general. Or it is a change in a process—that is, in how people work and produce something. Innovation therefore always has to be close to the market, focused on the market, indeed market-driven."

WHO ARE YOUR COMPETITORS?

Try to address this question in light of the previous subjects. That is, once you have defined your product as something unique, and established the customers or market you are selling to, you should be able to position your offering as something that your competitors can't easily knock off. What are you providing that others can't or won't?

You can't afford to be naïve about your odds for survival in the marketplace. Your reward for creating a terrific product or service will inevitably be a raft of competitors that target your prime customers. Why shouldn't they? If you've done great work in identifying an excellent product for a healthy market, why wouldn't any company strive to serve these customers as well? You need to be ruthless in assessing who else offers competitive products to that which you intend to sell. How is yours similar, and how is it different? Moreover, what are your comparative competitive strengths? That is, what advantages do you have in bringing something to market compared to them, and what will they always be able to do better?

Be imaginative when assessing the competition. Few printing shops imagined that Staples would one day appear on the scene and expand their services to include print services. Nor did local toy retailers expect to be trounced by Wal-Mart.

HOW WILL YOU PRODUCE YOUR PRODUCT OR SERVICE?

What will your venture require operationally? What type of equipment will you need? What skills? Can you go from making one of your products to making 100? How will you transport the goods? Are there materials that are difficult for you to track down? Essentially, you need to anticipate and plan for virtually every physical and logistical detail in producing your goods.

As an abstract exercise, answering this question can be extremely tough. You don't know exactly how you'll make the goods or run the store until you are actually doing it. So, the best way to get this information, and anticipate as much as possible about your business, is, quite simply, to crib from others. So, read other people's business plans. Not to copy ideas, per se, but to open your mind to all the factors you must address. Generally speaking, the best place to learn about market conditions, potential contingencies, financing needs, and all the minutiae that might confront your business is in the plans of others. There are many books, Web sites, peer groups, and other resources for business plans.

Consider also how you will reach your customers. What are the steps by which you can get your products sold to them? How can you market to them? Again, you need to speak with as many people as possible, limn the market, and come up with detailed plans that show exactly how you will reach your customers.

"When you plan your year and the strategies that will help you achieve your plan, detail and benchmarks are vital. It took us many years to discover that the lack of benchmarks caused stagnation. Goals are established to be hit and timelines are essential. The lack of the two is an easy formula for apathy and procrastination. Dividing and conquering is a great theme. Individual people must be responsible and accountable for hitting a manageable number of goals in a given period. Again, if you overload the plan for any one person, you will put them into the OVERPROMISE/UNDERDELIVER scenario. This is not fair. Give people goals that they can hit and map their course to the finish line."

—Tom First

WHAT RESOURCES DO YOU HAVE?

What is required for you to start delivering your offering to your customers? How much of it do you have in place and on hand? How
much time and energy will be required of you to gain control of those
remaining tools to deliver the goods? This is no simple area. Here you
have to spell out how you'll produce your product, how you'll reach
your customers, how you plan to crack the distribution channels.

Just who are you and what qualifies you to run a business? This
question is one of the first that potential investors will want to know.
"Strategy is easy, but tactics—the day-to-day and month-to-month
decisions required to manage a business—are hard. That's why I generally pay more attention to the people who prepare a business plan
than to the proposal itself," says veteran venture capitalist Arthur Rock,
when explaining why he always prefers to read about the people in a
venture more than studying the financial projections section. Investors
will want some kind of assurance that you have the experience, contacts, and skill set to run the business you propose, and may make their
decision about whether to fund your venture or not on that basis.

Now, you may or may not have sterling credentials—but let the
potential investors worry about that. For you, the salient question you
should consider as to whether you can create the company is this:
What *authority* do you have to run your company? Anybody can have
a good idea—yet that idea becomes compelling when put into practice by an individual who is uniquely suited to exploit it. As I've said
before, I believe that the process of running your business will teach
you what you need to know in order to succeed. Yet you must put
yourself in the position to succeed by becoming authoritative, not
merely about the industry you are competing in, but in every last

picayune detail that you can possibly learn that affects the success of your venture.

Consider immersing yourself in the business of your business before launching your own company. This way you can gather real information about how companies operate in this field, and you can also gauge whether you have the right skills for this particular startup. When Kate Mattes wanted to open a mystery bookstore, for example, she decided to recreate something called "field terms" at her college—which were essentially unpaid internships.

Mattes knew she wanted to open a mystery bookstore, but had no real experience in the field. She was a social worker by training, and had just inherited enough money to get started. "I just didn't know if I was looking to get out of my job, or if the bookstore was what I really wanted to do," she says. Through her brother, a literary agent, Mattes arranged an unpaid six-month apprenticeship at Otto Penzler's Mysterious Book Store in New York. In return for her free labor, Mattes was schooled in the details of the shop. She shelved books and ran the register and ordered from the publishers. This proved invaluable for Mattes when she opened her own mystery bookstore, Kate's Mystery Books, in 1983.

"I learned that there was a lot of physical labor involved, such as moving the books and keeping things systematized. I learned that carrying used books could be very profitable. I learned that there is not a good definition of mystery—and that I should carry authors like Tom Clancy, Stephen King, and other horror writers who are pure horror." And, best of all, Mattes says, the experience confirmed for her that she knew enough to strike out on her own. "I found that I did have enough skills and experience to run my own store," she says. Mattes, a lifetime mystery aficionado, knew enough about the books to give advice. Her background as a social worker helped her with customers finding what they liked. She realized that all this could come together for her store: "I knew I wanted to build a sense of community and found that I did have the skills to make it work."

Finally, you need to consider how you will compensate for what you *don't* know. This probably means tapping into others with more, or more impressive, or more relevant, experience than yours. Who else will be supporting your venture? Will they be teaming up with you as partners, advisors, unofficial board members? What skills and traits do they bring to the table that will compensate for skills and traits that you lack? This last question is the most important: You should always try to match up with partners, advisors, board members, and other supporters who complement your own skills.

EVOLVE

Finally, as you do the research to prepare your plan, always revise the document—but more importantly, constantly evolve your company as you learn what it takes. Use the process of creating a plan as a vehicle for knowing your industry cold—and then calibrating your venture accordingly. "Getting a business going takes a lot of baby steps and perseverance," says Laura Peck Fennema. "You take a step, analyze it, let it gel, and then go to the next."

As Fennema began to research how to bring her natural health and beauty products to market, she learned an enormous amount about what types of products were most successful and how she should adjust her wares accordingly. Spa owners, for example, told her that while her body massage oils were lovely, few people would use them regularly, and that she should concentrate on daily replenishment products. So Fennema developed body lotions, daily use hair products, and body gels. She evolved from making exotic types of concoctions that pleased her tastes to producing goods that she could sell regularly to a loyal group of customers.

Moreover, her ongoing conversations with spa directors paid off in another way. Fennema found that she could use many of their contacts to distribute her products to five star spa properties—a smart sales vehicle that gave her immediate access to the target audience, and shortened the sales cycle dramatically.

HOW DO YOU MAKE MONEY?

Of course, there's one small question we haven't addressed yet: how your business makes money. This topic merits an entire chapter—the next one. For now, suffice it to say that your planning must include a detailed financial summary of how your business makes money. At this point, don't obsess over the numbers; it's impossible at this point to have a realistic grasp of how your company will perform. But the key function of the financial tables is to demonstrate that you understand how your venture will make money, and are authoritative enough to pinpoint the key metrics that determine its health.

Remember to keep one thought in mind: When you prepare your plan, one traditional piece of advice is to write the last page, or exit

---

"I have come to believe that spreadsheets have an innate virus that infects the projections made in business plans. The virus turns what might be sensible people into wildly optimistic, nonsensical maniacs."

—Bill Sahlman, note on business plans

---

strategy, first. You may never intend to sell your company, yet you should always keep its value in mind nonetheless. Gauging your company's value in the market is a good way of keeping you honest. The dispassionate opinion of potential buyers reveals the flaws in your business, and helps you realize what is truly valuable. It forces you to think about the financial consequences of your decisions, and pushes you toward migrating into higher-value-adding behavior. (This topic is discussed in more detail in Chapter 3—see the resources listing at the end of Chapter 3, which include "Valuing Your Business" by Wilbur Yegge.)

"The best businesses are those in which you have large profit margins, you get paid by your customers before you have to deliver the product, and the fixed asset requirements are modest. It goes without saying, in addition, that such a business should be characterized by insuperable entry barriers."

—Bill Sahlman, *How to Write a Great Business Plan*

"What's wrong with most business plans? The answer is relatively straightforward. Most waste too much ink on numbers and devote too little to the information that really matters to intelligent investors . . . . Don't misunderstand me: business plans should include some numbers. But those numbers should appear mainly in the form of a business model that shows the entrepreneurial team has thought through the key drivers of the venture's success or failure. In manufacturing, such a driver might be the yield on a production process; in magazine publishing, the anticipated renewal rate; or in software, the impact of using various distribution channels."

—Bill Sahlman, *How to Write a Great Business Plan*

Now that you've done your planning, and used the process of answering these questions as an opportunity to hook up with customers and to start generating cash, here are a few additional thoughts.

Choose Wisely

Choose a business that matches up to your passion, but also choose one that has a great chance of succeeding. In *My Turn at Bat*, a wonderful memoir of his life as baseball's greatest hitter (okay, so I reveal my Red Sox heart), Ted Williams reveals the secret to his success: "To be a good hitter you've got to get a good ball to hit. It's the first rule in the book." Quick hands and great eyesight count for a lot— but true hitting success stems from developing the patience and confidence to swing only when the time is right. There's an obvious translation to business opportunity. It takes a lot more work to make a decent idea succeed than it does to start with a great one.

CEO James Marcus, for instance, cultivated patience and discernment when he launched University Angels, an online service that connects would-be entrepreneurs with prospective investors who have also graduated from the same universities. Marcus, who had worked for several companies prior to launching University Angels in 1999, says he learned the hard way to wait for what he calls "A" ideas—the ones that he has a high degree of confidence will work. Marcus had worked excruciatingly hard hours in turning around a company that made in-store promotional material; and he had worked that hard when running a company that acquired regional beverage distributors. With University Angels, he passed up thirty or forty opportunities because he had learned to wait for one without built-in obstacles. "My past companies taught me to be thorough up front and understand the company," he says. "I didn't want to be involved with any company that had a major challenge—one, for instance, that I glossed over simply because of enthusiasm for the business."

Of course it's impossible to know whether your business idea is a great one until you actually start doing business. The lesson here is to be willing to give up ideas that seem too much of a stretch, or be willing to evolve your original venture based on feedback that you are receiving from the business community.

FIND OUT MORE THAN YOU NEED TO KNOW

Be relentless and compulsive in gathering the detailed information you need on your company. Pay careful attention to those things that surprise you. The importance of understanding and anticipating details can't be underestimated. For example, when restaurateur Scott Shaw was researching potential costs for a restaurant, he found that a competitor had incurred extra costs when it was fined for using recorded music without paying royalties. Although they had inadvertently done so, this incident tipped Shaw off to an expense he would not have otherwise anticipated. These types of aberrations are the rule in startups, not the exception.

Stay Focused on Your Mission

Yes, seek profitable, cash-generating activities. But always keep your greater purpose in mind. "If the motivation in the early days is just money, it distorts your path and makes it harder to be successful," says co-founder Tom First of Nantucket Nectars. Consider the case of Bill Taylor and Alan Webber, the founders of the business magazine *Fast Company*. After leaving their posts at *Harvard Business Review* in

1992, the two decided to pursue their dream of launching a business magazine of their own. As a means of testing the waters, they launched a monthly newsletter of business ideas that they published for an elite audience of selected business leaders, at a super-premium cost. They wrote and published the report themselves. The two could have easily earned a generous income through this product, says Bill Taylor, but, ultimately, both were driven by a deep passion to produce a leading business magazine that provided something different than anything else that existed. And so they used their newsletter as a means of generating income, keeping in touch with key business leaders, and keeping in touch with leading business ideas while going through the long, although fruitful process, of creating *Fast Company*.

Be Flexible!

Yes, stay focused on your broader mission—but never get so tied down to your business plan that you lose sight of a great opportunity. Remember the corridor principle—that while you need goals and mission as a direction driving your enterprise, being in business will reveal opportunities you hadn't realized before. Listen to your customers, and stay attentive to what the market is telling you.

Okay. So at this point you've determined the shape and purpose of your company. You've used the planning process as a means of identifying your customers and of refining what you are offering. Now, as you begin to operate the company in earnest, you need to master the one discipline that drives even some veteran entrepreneurs crazy: financial literacy. Let's look at how to figure out how your business makes money, and what it needs as financial fuel.

"Having a superior product or service is a prerequisite to being in business. If it is not better than anything else you don't stand a chance."

—Gary Hirshberg, Stonyfield Farm

RESOURCES

Innovation and Entrepreneurship by Peter Drucker (HarperCollins, New York, 1985)

In this short though dense book, the preeminent management thinker of this century shares some of the most insightful thoughts anywhere on how entrepreneurial companies operate. While much of the book is aimed at managers who are now in large companies, Drucker's understanding of the sources of innovation is invaluable. Moreover, my very personal opinion is this: Chapter 15, simply titled "The New Venture," is the single most intelligent and useful analysis of what new ventures need that I've ever read.

Some Thoughts on Business Plans by William Sahlman

While this Harvard Business School case study (which was also published as an *HBR* article and included in the book *HBR on Entrepreneurship*) is primarily addressed at people seeking high-growth high-stakes companies, his framework for analyzing the key criteria in the success of new ventures is invaluable. Sahlman dispenses shrewd and lively insight on the factors that account for success (people first, then opportunity, external context, and the deal), while debunking conventional wisdom on the way ("on a scale of 1 to 10, business plans rank no higher than 2 as a predictor of likely success.")

Business Plans for Dummies by Paul Tiffany and Steven D. Peterson, (IDG Books, Foster City, California, 1997)

In this particular case, the title of this crisp book couldn't be farther from the truth. Tiffany and Peterson write in simple language and provide useful exercises, but they manage to cover a great deal of ground, ranging from sophisticated financial instruction to veiled references to such arcane fields of study as the diffusion of innovation. This book serves a helpful role in using the business plan as a discovery process for readying your enterprise.

Anatomy of a Business Plan by Linda Pinson and Jerry Jinnett, (Dearborn, Chicago, 1989)

This large-format workbook does a terrific job of explaining the various elements of a business plan. And it provides several detailed examples of completed plans by other companies. This guide serves as the best workbook for constructing a formal plan that meets the expectations of those who are counting on you to observe the details of this exercise.

3

The Numbers That Count

"Annual income twenty pounds, annual expenditures
nineteen nineteen six, result happiness.
Annual income twenty pounds, annual expenditures
twenty pounds ought and six, result misery."
—Micawber, in Charles Dickens' *David Copperfield*

LEARN FINANCIAL LITERACY

David Schwartz grew up in a book-selling family. His father, Harry W. Schwartz, founded Milwaukee's best-known string of bookstores and passed it on to his son. Yet David, who spent his youth stocking books and talking titles with customers, didn't become the owner of the store simply by absorbing its assets. David only learned to manage with a sense of control when he mastered the key numbers of how the company made money.

His lesson came by necessity rather than choice. In 1984, the company's lack of financial structures led it to the brink of extinction, a condition that forced David to start running the business by the numbers. In particular, this meant that David, who loved books, learned to see them as more (or less) than venerated cultural artifacts. He learned to see them as *inventory*. Prior to the financial crisis, David was what he called a "macho buyer," who would purchase large numbers of books he felt that customers should buy—and let them sit in the warehouse while waiting for consumer taste to catch up. When his new partner, Avin Domnitz, pointed out the cost of such excess inventory, they began a more responsive system for moving their product through their stores. And, more importantly, they began to make all their business decisions through a clearer financial lens.

Sooner or later all business owners must learn Schwartz's enforced discipline. As your business gets going, you will learn the prime importance of understanding how your particular venture makes money. This key measure drives virtually every key decision you make. It forces you to address everything from how you price your product to what type of margins you seek. What activities can you handle within your company, and what should you outsource? Knowing where your money comes from and where it goes informs how much capital you need to raise and who you tap for this investment, how many employees you can afford to hire, and even how you should use your time.

The best metaphor may be that of an automobile. Learning how to use your company's financial numbers as a dashboard, a set of indicators of health, literally puts you in the driver's seat of your company. You can take your car out of the driveway without looking at the dashboard, but you shouldn't drive anywhere without checking your speed limit and gas gauge. Likewise with your business, you need to be constantly aware of the simple measures of financial health. Keeping track of the right numbers helps you tie every decision to the bottom line of your company and provides you with a more integrated understanding of how things fit together.

You need more than a simple understanding of how money flows through your company as a sustaining force. In all likelihood, you will also need to secure capital for your business. It may be your own, or that of friends and family; it may come from a bank or another

---

"You can't start a company until you decide how to finance it, and the financing decisions you make along the way will forever affect how you approach your business. Should you dig deep into your pockets, take a second mortgage on your house, visit generous relatives and fill out as many credit card applications as you can get your hands on? That's a good choice if your priority is to remain king of your company, doing whatever you want, whenever you want, and not answering to anybody.

"But, suppose you're staring at a huge opportunity that you just can't pursue through these traditional methods of financing—an idea that requires large quantities of capital coupled with rapid growth in order to reach fruition. Big ideas are rarely grown to a large scale through the incremental growth path of the traditional small business. Many of today's hottest public companies that are less than 10 years old reached their present size via multiple rounds of private equity financing—with entrepreneurs selling pieces of their business along the way."

—Martin Babinec, *The Impact of Equity on Personal Wealth*

---

lending institution. Such money always comes with a set of rules and mutual expectations. To secure and use this money wisely, you need to be aware of the rules that govern how you qualify for money, the implicit and explicit expectations of investors, and the tradeoffs surrounding your fiscal decisions. What's more, the issues of how much money you raise, and how you make money, are fundamentally tied together.

Ultimately, financial literacy in a small business comes down to this: understanding how your decisions translate into the key financial measures of your company's health, and basing your decisions on those numbers. Naturally, you are pursuing something beyond mere profit with your enterprise—but, as we discussed in Chapter 1, "Finding Your Calling," your business certainly exists to maximize profits. This chapter will help you become financially literate by finding and applying the key numbers for your business.

This chapter also looks at how you become proficient at garnering the resources you need for your business. Asking for financial support for your company involves *simply asking for help*. Just as selling comes naturally to some entrepreneurs, so too does asking others for support. Yet, for some of you, asking for money invokes terror. Understanding the ground rules and the tradeoffs involved can help make this process easier.

At this point in your business, you have taken your first steps toward operating your business. You have defined your product and begun your transactions with customers. You have determined how you will deliver your goods and have an understanding of the value you add in this exchange. Now, as you become operational, you must build in financial controls and develop financial literacy as an operating principle.

"If finance is useful to general managers of large firms, it is especially useful to entrepreneurs, for they are the ultimate general managers, responsible for making many, if not most, of the decisions in their enterprises. Entrepreneurs are value creators, investing today in hopes of generating cash flows tomorrow. They must understand what cash flow will do; they must understand and manage risk; they must understand how value is determined. Indeed, the importance of thinking through problems from the finance perspective is probably even more important for entrepreneurial firms than it is for larger companies. A key goal of the entrepreneur must be to keep playing the game; ignoring finance risks being forced to stop playing."

—Bill Sahlman, "The Financial Perspective:
What Should Entrepreneurs Know?"
The Entrepreneurial Venture (HBS Publishing)

ACKNOWLEDGE THE RULES

In his lovely book *The Seven Laws of Money*, author and financial veteran Michael Phillips says, "money has its own rules." One of the most powerful laws concerning money states that you must pay close attention to this abstract stuff. As Phillips says, "The first and clearest rule is that you have to keep track of your money. You have to know approximately how much you have, how much you are spending, how much is coming in, and what the general direction of your dollar flow is." Phillips says that to make good decisions you don't always need to know your net worth to the penny on a daily basis, but you should be generally aware of how much you are spending and how much you are receiving. Although Phillips is discussing personal finance, his point is eminently germane to your business.

To keep track of your company's finances, you need to respect the language of money. Bankers and accountants use an elaborate and often opaque language with which to discuss money. Every businessperson who deals with them—this means you—is expected to understand the fundamentals to take part in the conversation. Please forgive the following digression into the more formal aspects of business accounting. At the end of this chapter, I refer to several terrific books that delve into much greater detail of these aspects, and I highly recommend that you read them. At the bare minimum, you need to understand the following basics.

Folks who speak the language of finance use three financial statements: the income statement, the balance sheet, and cash flow. Each set of numbers tracks a different function. Each one is important for your business. (Note: I highly recommend the terrific book *Managing by the Numbers* by Chuck Kremer et al.—see "Resources" at the end of the chapter.)

The *balance sheet* provides what experts call a "snapshot" of your business's financial condition at one particular point in time. Think of this statement as what your business owns and what it owes. This statement lists your assets (what the business owns or is due), your liabilities (what the business owes), and the difference between assets and liabilities, which is called the owner's equity. This sheet is constructed so that your assets minus your liabilities necessarily equal the owner's equity; thus, when it is produced correctly, the sums are balanced.

The *income statement* tracks your company's profitability over a given period of time. It says whether, in a specific period, you made money or didn't. But, and this is a huge *but*, it's an abstraction. It shows the promises that people have made to pay you money, and the agreements you have made to pay others. "It shows whether you're making money on the goods or services you provide, once you have taken all your costs and expenses into account. But it isn't real," write Kremer et al. "It doesn't show how much cash you put in your bank account or how much cash you spent." Income statements are subject to manipulation. Because income statements are affected by intangible factors such as depreciation (which tracks how an asset loses value over time), you can show a profit—or loss—that is not directly tied to your activities in that span of time. Moreover, income statements count promises that others have made to pay you as actual income, while the daily reality may be quite different. So, these statements indicate profitability—which is good—but they don't necessarily reflect your daily, actual situation.

For that you have *cash flow*. Cash flow is, very simply, the difference between your cash receipts and your cash expenditures. It's what you have left after you spend the money that you take in. Consider this measure to be your business checkbook: what cash is actually coming into your business and what is actually being spent? There's no fudging cash. It's what you have on hand—the balance in your account.

Even though all three numbers matter for your company, one towers over the others as the most important: cash, cash, cash.

"In the startup phase, there's really only one exercise that you need to know, and that is cash flow," says CEO Gary Hirshberg of Stonyfield Farm. "Some people take issue with this. They say you need to know your income statement and your balance sheet because that helps you understand your borrowing abilities. That might be true —but the most important thing you have to know is when you are going to run out of cash. Everything else is irrelevant."

"Entrepreneurs starting new ventures are rarely unmindful of money; on the contrary, they tend to be greedy. They therefore focus on profits. But this is the wrong focus for a new venture, or rather, it comes last rather than first. Cash flow, capital, and controls come much earlier. Without them, the profit figures are fiction—good for twelve to eighteen months, after which they evaporate.

"Growth has to be fed. In financial terms this means that growth in a new venture demands adding financial resources rather than taking them out. Growth needs more cash and more capital. If the growing venture shows a 'profit' it is a fiction: a bookkeeping entry put in only to balance the accounts. And since taxes are payable on this fiction in most countries, it creates a liability and a cash drain rather than 'surplus.' The healthier a new venture and the faster it grows, the more financial feeding it requires . . . .

"The new venture needs cash flow analysis, cash flow forecasts, and cash management. The fact that America's new ventures of the last few years (with the significant exception of high-tech companies) have been doing so much better than new ventures used to do is largely because the new entrepreneurs in the United States have learned that entrepreneurship demands financial management."

—Peter Drucker, *Entrepreneurship and Innovation,* p. 194

"Sales do not equal cash, and cash is what you need to survive. You run out of cash, you go out of business. End of story."

—Norm Brodsky

Understanding cash flow represents the first step toward managing by the numbers, says Hirshberg. "You have to expedite what is coming and slow down what is going out. Financial literacy comes down to nothing more than knowing what the big nuts are and how to stretch them," he says.

Sounds simple, sure. But odds are that in your early days you will be tempted to track your financial health by another number: pure sales. Getting new customers and making sales is intoxicating for any entrepreneur—which is why one of the hardest challenges is to move from a sales mentality to a positive cash flow mentality. "At the early stage, you often think of revenue as the one critical number. When you are beginning, the only thing you are thinking about is how to increase sales," says founder Martin Babinec of Trinet. What gets lost, says Babinec, is a hard-headed look at the growing costs of getting and fulfilling those sales. "At some point, you need to look at how to grow that stream while looking at the numbers coming in and going out."

Ignore this figure at great risk. "The failure to look at cash flow will likely result in infant mortality for your business," Babinec says. The key to avoiding this trap is to build in a reporting system that tracks your cash. "If you run your business on a balance sheet rather than a checkbook, you get into cash flow problems. You are counting your receivables as cash—but they are not cash. You have customers who are not paying you. Your accounts receivable are not on your checkbook, but they are on your balance sheet. And suddenly the world closes in. Suddenly, you are in over your head. This is what drags companies under. The earlier you develop some accounting systems (usually with outside help) that manage the cash flow of your business from day one, the better off your chances of success will be."

"I learned, during those dark early days, that I had to do a daily cash flow," says Hirshberg, who lived in constant fear of the company dying from lack of cash. "Calculating your cash on this constant basis, and knowing when you are going to run out is a bit like driving in the fog. It forces you to focus on the road right ahead of you," he says. To provide this financial headlight, Hirshberg created a simple format for calculating his own cash on hand, which he revised daily. (See the sidebar "The Daily Cash Flow Equation.")

In fact, he considers his grounding in daily cash flow as the basis for becoming knowledgeable in the other key statements and their implications. "The income statement and the balance sheet are obviously important, but you learn about them as a consequence of steeling in your bones the cash flow," he says. "When you know where your money is flowing then the rest is easy to fix and manage. And getting debt, or equity, is just another way of getting a cash infusion to cover a shortfall."

Understanding the immediate implications of cash at hand dramatically changed Hirshberg's approach to raising capital. He stopped going out and chasing it from investors and took a more disciplined look at the activities that Stonyfield could afford to conduct on its own. "My background was in raising money for nonprofits—and the company probably would have been better off if it wasn't," Hirshberg

THE DAILY CASH FLOW EQUATION

For the first decade of his company's operation, Gary Hirshberg would track cash flow on a daily basis using this simple formula. On the left-hand side he would start with his beginning balance, and then put down income below that. Income would be broken down into two parts: sales and investments (borrowings or equity.) Then below that he would list expenses, including milk, labor, packaging, and fruit. At the bottom he could then calculate the operating balance (income plus expenses), and at the end he would have the end balance. This end balance at the day's close would be the beginning balance for the next day.

jokes today. Because he *could* raise money from outsiders, he did. He thus spent more time on this activity than necessary, diverting his attention from critical internal decisions. At one key juncture, Hirshberg approached a dairy in Vermont to ask for support in building a plant to manufacture yogurt. After long negotiations and complications, the deal fell through. And then Hirshberg ended up coming up with a different solution: securing an SBA loan and building the factory himself. "If I had been more disciplined in tracking our cash, I might have spared us a lot of trouble," he says.

RAISING MONEY

Hirshberg's revelation about how the numbers relate is crucial. I began this chapter by going into how your business is making money before talking about how much you need to raise. For some of you, this may seem backwards, especially because you may need to raise money in order to get your business going. There's a reason for this structure. And it is quite simply this. *You can't understand how much you need if you don't know how your business makes money.* Understanding your operating expenses and cash flow enables you to choose the right source and amount of capital that your business needs. Your business planning should have given you a sense of all the various costs your business requires, and your development of financial literacy tells you how to feed the various needs of your business.

Okay, so now you face a major challenge for many startups: raising capital. Now, before we delve into this topic, let me make a few more points. The first is to examine whether you actually need to raise investment money *at all*. If you are a service business, for example, and don't need to buy materials to prepare, or if you have some means of leveraging resources to get you going without a major investment —then by all means do so. Just as the quest for the perfect business plan can keep you from your real business, so too can an unnecessary chase for capital. The next chapter talks about bootstrapping, or the art of leveraging your existing resources. Developing self-sufficiency and frugal management go hand in hand with financial literacy.

What you need to do is run through your numbers and determine, with a cold eye, whether or not you need investment capital. If you don't, then great. Move on to the next chapter.

Now, many startups do need capital to get going. It's a fact of business life. And other young or growing companies need a capital infusion to feed their growth. If you are producing products, for example, you need capital to buy the goods, and if you are opening a restaurant, you need to buy equipment and rent space and hire help. There's no argument with that.

If you do, your first challenge is to find the right amount and the right source. Every particular business has its own set of financial needs, and a careful owner should tap the source of capital that matches the company's particular needs. Whether you should seek venture capital, angel investing, a bank loan, or a simple private investor depends on the nature of your business and your long-term plans. A restaurant owner doesn't need venture capital, just as a high-tech startup can't last without significant investments from equity partners. Each business differs by industry, strategy, character, and resources. Why should its capital needs be cookie-cutter?

Your financial needs change as your business grows, and you will need to recalibrate your source and structure of finance accordingly. When, for example, restaurateur Scott Shaw was growing the Austin Grill restaurant chain in Austin, Texas, and Washington, D.C.,

---

"The big-money model has little in common with the traditional low-budget startup. Raising big money requires careful market research, well thought-out business plans, top-notch founding teams, sagacious boards, quarterly performance reviews, and devilishly complex financial structures. It is an environment in which analytical, buttoned-down professionals can make a seamless transition from the corporate world to the world of the entrepreneur. It is not the world of the entrepreneur."

—Amar Bhide, "Bootstrap Finance," Nov.–Dec. 1992 HBR, reprinted in *HBR on Entrepreneurship* (p. 151)

---

he used four different sources and models of investment to grow the business—each one appropriate for his particular needs at the time. (See the sidebar "Different Needs, Different Deals.")

Your deals will probably not be as complex. But let's start at the beginning. Have you determined how much you need? This number should be derived from your operating assumptions about the business. Have you considered every possible expense, every contingency? Use your plan, your projections, and your understanding of how your business operates to derive a sum that will meet your needs.

Don't ask for too much capital. Not only will this hurt your chances, but you may also suffer by succeeding at this goal. Too much capital? Yes, you can have that problem. There are two flaws. First, it costs money to carry. You have to swap something for this money —whether a stake in the company or excessive carrying costs on the loan. Neither is particularly attractive for a startup. And second, it can give you a false sense of security that enables you to waste money on big offices and expensive gadgets rather than force you to remain

It's key to seek the right source of capital and the right type of deal that match your company's needs at the time.

Consider how restaurateur Scott Shaw and his partners stepped up the nature and amount of financing to match the growth of their company. As the Austin Grill grew, so too did its financial needs. Here's how the founders designed deals that were good fits at different stages of growth. When Shaw launched the company, he and his friends raised the funds from their friends and family. As the business grew and they launched a second site, Shaw and his partners financed the expansion by bringing in private investors in a limited partnership. The company continued to grow, and when they opened more new locations, Shaw and his partners issued preferred stock tied to the performance of the grills. Finally, as the Austin Grill continued to add more locations, the partners launched a direct public offering of shares.

focused on your core business. Fact is, you need the capital to become cash-flow positive on your operations, pure and simple. Don't ever lose sight of that. So, be like Goldilocks. Not too much, not too little. Find the amount that is just right.

WHERE DO YOU GO?

Roughly speaking, investments break down into two forms: debt and equity. You take on debt when you borrow money from a lender and pay interest on that investment. You are compelled to repay the money with interest over time. Or, you can take on an equity

WHAT DO INVESTORS WANT?

Inviting others to invest in your business creates significant new responsibilities for you. Although many of these brave souls care deeply about seeing you succeed personally, never forget what's at the heart of this transaction: your investors are pledging their financial support in return for a reasonable return on their capital.

Naturally, you will form different deals with different investors. Some investors, such as family members, may be extremely patient with their capital and expect some form of payout far down the road. Others may be counting on regular payments. Some individuals may ask for a stake in your company and expect you to grow by leaps and bounds right away—in line with their big score!

Regardless of the individual deal you cut, there's one overriding principle when it comes to investors: be crystal clear about their goals and expectations, and your company's realistic ability to meet them. Their risk must be aligned with the reasonable return they can expect, based on an honest assessment of your company, and a knowledge of your future plans. You have to calibrate their tolerance for risk with the course you plan on taking with the company. If they expect a safe investment that will provide them with regular dividends, they may be chagrined if your company burns up its cash by chasing high-risk projects.

Such explicit conversations about mutual goals are even more important when you are dealing with individuals for whom personal and professional issues are already blurred. Given that you have probably asked friends and family for help, defining the risks and possible returns on the investment capital are even more important. It's very possible that things

continues

WHAT DO INVESTORS WANT? (*continued*)

will not turn out as planned, and having everyone understand why from the beginning lessens the prospect of lingering resentment over deals gone bad.

Such a conversation should never end. Once your business gets operational, you must keep your investors appraised of current conditions. You don't have to tell them about every sale or setback, but you do need to keep them tuned into the key measures of health for the business.

---

investment—in which you sell a portion of the company to an investor in return for cash or something else of value.

Each source has its advantages and disadvantages. Consider them well before making choices, because finance decisions are hard to undo. It's not enough to find lenders and investors; you have to pick the right ones. Try to find investors who bring more than cash to the table. Look for supporters who can help you with financial advice or technical assistance, or who can connect you with key customers. Seek patient capital from a sage who can listen to your problems over breakfast and set you straight by the time you reach the office.

Also, make sure that you find investors whose interests align with yours. Naturally, anyone who lends you money is betting on the success of the company, but be sure that you have clear mutual goals and agree about what those goals are and when they will be reached. If you are going to friends or family, for example, make sure that they are not investing money that must be repaid in a few months. Also, be clear with others what your long-term goals are. You don't want to surprise investors if you eschew rapid growth, or make other decisions that are consistent with your vision, yet don't reconcile with theirs.

"Capital raising should be an extending circle," says Scott Shaw. He explains that you start small with an immediate group of investors who can help you directly. Then you gradually build on that platform, seeking larger amounts from people you come to meet and with whom you will probably have a more formal relationship. Shaw also counsels that you "listen to the capital markets." They may be trying to tell you something about your venture. If you're having trouble raising money, there may be a very good reason why. If you are going out to seek capital—and the associated advice—from people who may have more experience, it's a good idea to listen to them! They may know something you don't.

So, what are your capital choices? Let's start with simple loans. Your first source of capital will probably be a loan from yourself. Most businesses are founded with cash from the founder's pocketbook. Sure, simple advantages exist here: pure control and ownership. You own the whole company, control the show, and stand to reap the gains should your venture become valuable. Great.

But there's a huge potential downside here as well. Even the best-researched and most well-run startups involve risk. And you are putting your assets on the line. It's great to read about risk-takers who take out second mortgages on their homes and borrow from their retirement funds to launch businesses that turn them into millionaires. The news contains far fewer stories about the many people who take great risks—and fail. And, unfortunately, these stories are very real and very common. So although I believe you need to trust yourself, and take the leap, be sure to consider (and reconsider!) the risk of your venture carefully when investing your own money.

Wild stories have been told of individuals who turn to credit cards for their startup capital. Sure, in our credit-easy economy, credit cards represent an easy form of quick cash, one that many starting entrepreneurs exploit—especially when they come with low rates. Yet the eventual high rates and lack of any other support rank them low on the list of sources.

The next most popular source of loans for startups comes from friends and family. On the plus side, loans from such intimate ties can be a blessing, a sign of love and confidence. They may have generous terms, and they might be easily obtainable. But keep in mind: they too come with strings attached. Wait—let me put it another way: they come with ropes attached—huge, hairy ropes that are potentially agonizing because they are so hidden from plain view. Many entrepreneurs who tap their parents or friends for capital find that they have created a vehicle called a business that enables them to recreate old conflicts or relationships. You will have to feed their emotional investment as well as their financial one. Such costs can greatly devalue the value of your loan. Try to borrow from those with whom you know your relationship will withstand the failure of your business.

The key thing here is to realize that when they give you money, they're not just friends and family—they're investors. Loans from a friend or family member should be handled less formally, right? No need to be too nit-picky about terms of repayment or other such legal stuff, right? Wrong. In fact, you can't be too careful about writing down the terms that come with a loan from someone with whom you have deep emotional ties. You need to be clear up front about how much risk is going into this investment, and to create a formal document that prepares for the contingencies that may arise. Such a document can save a lot of grief if you have trouble repaying the loan.

Of course, hard feelings may arise, regardless of preparations, should you fail to repay the loan. There's not much to say except . . . don't let this happen.

The next circle of support is <u>outside investors</u>: individuals who believe you have the ability to deliver on your promises and are seeking a decent return on their money. Bear in mind that you should think expansively about potential investors (see the sidebar "Customers as Investors.") Cast a wide net. Ask everyone who knows and does business with your business whether they want the opportunity *to invest* in your business. Build on the circle of contacts that you have or are forming with your business. Remember that you are building networks, so if one person cannot help you with money, thank them for their consideration, and ask if they know others who could.

From here, you launch into more formal territory, starting with banks. Many small business owners feel that banks lend them money only after they become financially solvent, or, in other words, when they least need the capital. There's an element of truth here. Because one of the key pieces of information banks look for when considering a loan is a demonstration of cash flow, they are not necessarily the best source for starting funds. Nonetheless, you are well served to cultivate a good relationship with a banker in order to prepare yourself for a time when they can lend you money, and see whether they can provide you with advice or contacts in the meantime. (See the sidebar "What Bankers Want.")

Moreover, more banks today, especially smaller, community-based banks, are willing and able to help startups. The advantages of community banks are many: they provide short- to medium-term funding and are the single largest source of loans to small businesses and entrepreneurs. They "get" you and are often more flexible than

CUSTOMERS AS INVESTORS

Sometimes your best investors may be literally under your nose. Consider customers, vendors, and other individual relationships you have formed over the course of your business as potential investors. Such individuals bring to the table a healthy knowledge of the business, a willingness to share the risk, and a commitment to your success.

This type of community helped Sheldon McArthur buy a mystery bookstore in Los Angeles when the New York-based owner decided to shut down the sister site. At the time, McArthur was the long-term general manager of The Mysterious Bookshop West when owner Otto Penzler of the original Mysterious Bookshop in New York decided to close it down.

"My first thought was, 'My God, my life is over,'" says McArthur, a lifelong bookseller and perhaps one of the nation's leading experts on hard-boiled mysteries. "Then I thought, there has to be some alternative to closing the store." He called a longtime customer, attorney Ed Kaufman, who owned his own store, M is for Mystery, in San Mateo. Kaufman's advice: ask Penzler for a little time, find some investors, and buy the store.

McArthur turned to his customers for help. He sent an email to 500 names, asking for help in keeping the store open. Within two weeks, he had more potential investors than he needed. "We had, at one point, probably 60 potential investors. Once we had a business prospectus and plan . . . we sent that out," McArthur says. Kaufman spoke to each potential investor "to make sure that they really knew what this was about, that this would be a long-term investment."

continues

CUSTOMERS AS INVESTORS (*continued*)

As a result of this outpouring of support, McArthur's group was able to buy the store debt-free, and the store never closed its doors, seamlessly becoming The Mystery Bookstore in April 2000. The entire process—from the announcement that the store would close to the purchase of the Mysterious Bookshop West by Sheldon McArthur, LLC, and a group of 13 investors—took only 45 days.

In addition to providing startup capital, the store's investors provide legal and accounting services, Web site design and support, some retail and human resources advice, and sweat equity, helping physically move the store to a new location in Westwood Village. Mystery author and customer Charles Knief was the general contractor for the new store, and another long-time customer found a master carpenter to build the new store's shelves and fixtures.

"Without the incredible support of my customers turned into investors, I would not have had the financial support necessary to go independent," McArthur says. "My customers are my single greatest resource—besides buying books, they've provided resources, advice, public relations help . . . all, it seems, from a love of the store."

large institutions. Because they are smaller, your business is more important to them. And good community bankers often offer good advice and valuable contacts.

Don't forget that the government can help your small business. The *Small Business Administration* (SBA) offers a number of loans for startups. Actually, the SBA loans don't come directly from the SBA; this governmental agency guarantees a loan that you

WHAT BANKERS WANT

When President and CEO Bill McGurk of the Rockville Bank in Rockville, Connecticut, considers a small business loan application, "The key thing for me is what the applicants know about the business," he says, "People need to solidly know what they are getting into." McGurk wants to know that the business owners are aware of exactly what it takes to operate a successful business in this field. Recently, he granted a loan to a couple who were opening a bed and breakfast not on the basis of their current jobs—he was a carpenter and she a teacher. He was favorably disposed largely because her family had run a bed and breakfast on Nantucket. "She knew she wasn't going to be able to take weekends off," he said.

Another sign that loan applicants understand the nature of their business comes when they ask for the right amount, says McGurk. "We've had people come in and want to do half the job, buy half the loaf," he says. Those who ask for $15,000 when they need $30,000 reveal a naïvete about the business in particular, or their own business skills.

McGurk also gauges loans by character, which he defines as the ability and willingness to repay the loan for which you are applying. Your personal finances are Exhibit A in this area. "They've got to be solvent in their own right," says McGurk. He prefers that startup borrowers keep their day jobs (ensuring some cash flow to repay the loan) and ease into the new venture. "We want to be sure that there's a transition period."

Of course, bankers also like to see that you are putting your own capital into the venture. "People need to know that the bank is not your partner but your lender," says Roxanne Coady. "They need to know that you

continues

are putting your own money on the line. Why would they lend to you if you aren't taking some of the risk yourself? After all, you are the owner."

Finally, in lieu of actual experience, McGurk looks for authority—a clear demonstration that you've thought through the elements of your business. In this regard, a solid business plan helps tremendously. "Requirements for a business plan vary with a person's experience," he says. "Someone who really knows what he or she is doing can get away with a more basic business plan."

secure from any number of traditional lending institutions. The range of programs is too varied to go into here—but check out the Web site (**www.sba.gov**) for more information. Moreover, as I discussed in Chapter 2, "Planning as Learning, Learning as Doing," the agency that provides the loan is more than likely to offer education and services that will nourish your company. Whichever program you explore, be sure to look into the network of support that you can connect with in finding the capital. (See the sidebar "Sources of Capital, Sources of Support.")

EQUITY OR NOT?

Now, should you need more, or different, capital for your company, you will be faced with a decision that often proves agonizing for entrepreneurs: taking on equity financing. In other words, selling a portion of their beloved startups to investors in return for the resources to grow faster or healthier.

SOURCES OF CAPITAL, SOURCES OF SUPPORT

Every loan comes with an implied promise and an embedded pledge of support. So, whether you are seeking angel money or micro-enterprise seed capital, explore the ability of the lending institution (or individual) to help your particular enterprise. Here are a few sources of help.

ACCION International (**www.accionusa.org**) is the world's leading micro-enterprise lender, with offices in Albuquerque, Atlanta, Chicago, New York, San Antonio, and San Diego. ACCION lends specifically to low-income entrepreneurs, making loans from $500 to $50,000.

The **Angel Capital Network** (**https://ace-net.sr.unh.edu/pub/**) is a nonprofit Internet network that matches startup businesses with potential investors.

Community Development Financial Institutions (CDFI) are institutions that exist to promote economic growth in low- and moderate-income areas. They may be for-profit or nonprofit institutions, and often provide a great deal of mentoring and technical assistance in addition to funding. You can find a list of these institutions at **www.cdfi.org**, the home page of the Coalition of Community Development Financial Institutions.

"Accepting equity financing forever alters your entrepreneurial journey, because you no longer have the luxury of thinking about yourself as the primary recipient of the company's financial success," says CEO Martin Babinec of Trinet. However, accepting equity capital can help you grow fast, beyond what you might accomplish with your limited resources.

Yet many entrepreneurs find this decision emotionally challenging. First-time founders rarely like the idea of sharing their new venture. You've poured yourself into it, are emotionally wrapped up in the company, and fear that you will give away your investment and lose control of the company. Such emotions often impair your ability to make this decision rationally.

The important consideration to keep in mind, however, is the tradeoffs involved when you accept equity finance. You are exchanging a share of your business for an ownership stake with a new party, and they bring certain expectations to the table. You must be clear about what they are and anticipate how you will serve them under any circumstance. One of the key tradeoffs to consider is this: in terms of value, is it better to own a big piece of a small pie, or a larger piece of a smaller pie? Selling equity may diminish your actual stake in the venture but enable the company to grow much larger.

There's no magic formula for determining when to bring in investors, if at all. "My theory on equity is that you push as hard as you can to make your company as valuable as you can before you bring in equity—and then you bring it in," says Roxanne Coady of R. J. Julia Books.

Finally, should your business have the good fortune to grow, and grow quickly, your financial options will grow to include a variety of exotic and exciting offerings. See "Resources" at the end of the chapter for more details.

You may have noticed that venture capital hasn't been discussed. In today's culture, *venture capital* (VC) has garnered the cachet of success. Journalists and high-tech entrepreneurs obsess over who's who in the VC community and how much seed capital they are staking in burgeoning companies. Yet few companies qualify for venture capital, and rightly so. It tends to be "impatient money" held by stakeholders who snap up a large percentage of the company with the hopes of a quick profit from a company that grows at hyperspeed. You may belong to that miniscule subset of high-growth, high-tech companies with great promise to grow insanely fast and deliver great wealth to all involved. If so, I salute you. But for most small businesses, venture capital is a high-profile, high-headache, and, ultimately, low-probability source.

Okay, here are a few last thoughts on becoming financially literate.

DEVELOP YOUR OWN KEY NUMBER

Managing by the numbers helps you develop a form of shorthand. That is, learning how your company makes money enables you to isolate a "key number" that reveals the health of your company. All businesses have key gauges of the company's health. Booksellers may parse inventory turnover, attorneys use billable hours, and financial companies scrutinize "share of wallet," or how much of their client's financial transactions they handle. By analyzing your cash flow and operating budget, you can determine a key figure by which you can make fundamental decisions. I can't say the exact number that works for you, but try to come up with a simple, easy-to-track number that helps keep you focused on the right things.

BE HONEST WITH MONEY

Finally, the issue of money forces you to reconcile your business dreams with the daily reality of your company. You can fudge certain intangibles about your business, but when you run out of cash, you are out of business. So save the rosy scenarios for sales pitches. Be careful to plan for all possible expenses, prepare for slower than expected sales, and be able to find new sources of capital, if necessary.

Now you've got a sense of how your particular business makes money and how you can get your hands on this fundamental resource. Spending wisely ties into the next critical skill you must master—that of bootstrapping.

RESOURCES

Small Time Operator by Bernard Kamoroff, CPA (Bell Springs Publishing, revised annually, Willits, California.)

This is my all-time favorite resource for divining the critical information needed when it comes to your startup's basic details. Kamoroff is an accountant by training, and his best advice comes from his mastery of the fundamentals of a small business's primary financial requirements. Although he is crankily insightful on basic issues such as whether you should start a business in the first place, he is virtually all-knowing on such key matters as keeping the books, paying your taxes, and tracking cash flow. This is a great book for advice on keeping your books.

Managing by the Numbers by Chuck Kremer and Ron Rizzuto with John Case (Perseus Publishing, Cambridge, Massachusetts, 2000)

This gem limns the theory and practice of financial management for small companies. Set aside the fact that some of the basics may apply to larger or slightly more mature companies than yours. Read this to understand how to use the financial life of your company as the basis for critical operational decisions. Kremer et al. show how you need to understand three financial statements (the balance sheet,

the income statement, and cash flow) to truly evaluate your company's performance. Moreover, you really start to control this function when you learn how the three statements fit together.

The Great Game of Business by Jack Stack with Bo Burlingham (Doubleday Currency, New York, 1992)

"The best, most efficient, most profitable way to operate a business is to give everybody in the company a voice in saying how the company makes money and a stake in the financial outcome, good or bad," writes Stack. He goes on to explain how his company, Springfield Remanufacturing, has pioneered the practice of "open book management," in which employees are taught how the company makes money and are then charged with contributing individually. Though aimed at larger organizations, Stack's book is an excellent primer on how to find and communicate the right numbers for your company, and, more importantly, how to make financial literacy for all into an operating managerial practice.

Self-Defense Finance for Small Businesses by Wilbur M. Yegge (John Wiley & Sons, New York, 1995)

By far the least reader-friendly of the lot, Yegge's dense primer still merits a place on your shelf. That's because he always places his financial lectures in the context of how you will use the tools. What could feel like an academic text becomes an invitation to become more financially adept. His appendix on tips for negotiating justifies the cost of the book.

Angel Investing: Matching Startup Funds with Startup Companies

A Guide for Entrepreneurs and Investors by Mark Van Osnabrugge and Robert J. Robinson (Jossey-Bass Publishing, San Francisco, 2000)

A terrific guide for tapping into one of the most useful forms of investors: so-called angel investors. Although a trifle academic, this book still delivers a wise lesson to entrepreneurs in how to locate, secure, and use angel investors. I like the book for two primary reasons. First, it emphasizes that different companies have different capital needs, and it helps readers understand how to pick the source and amount that are right for them. And second, the authors provide a comprehensive appendix of resources to help you locate existing angel networks.

The Seven Laws of Money by Michael Phillips (Shambala, Boston, 1993)

"Do it!" Phillips says. "Money will come when you are doing the right thing." That's the first law in this simple, spirited, and hugely insightful guide to money from the man who developed MasterCard as a vice president of the Bank of California. Phillips helps reveal the neuroses and emotions that money triggers in individuals, and provides a lovely, soulful context to the ways in which people relate to this intangible force. Above all, Phillips provides a nice insight into the role money should and shouldn't play in pursuit of bigger things.

4

Bootstrapping

I've given you sunlight/I've given you rain
Looks like you're not happy/'less I open a vein
I'll give you a few drops/if that'll appease
Now please—oh please—grow for me.
—Seymour, *Little Shop of Horrors*

LEARN TO LEVERAGE YOUR MONEY, RESOURCES, TOOLS, CONTACTS, AND PASSION

Ann Handley and Andy Bourland have learned how to build a business out of thin air. In 1997 these two friends launched their company ClickZ by creating a simple Web site where people could learn about marketing on the Internet. The need arose when Bourland, who worked in business development for an Internet company, was frustrated with the lack of information on how to market online.

Over the next three years, they grew the company by operating cheaply, pouring their profits back into growth, and always expanding within their means. They grew into a company of twenty employees with sales of nearly $8 million annually without taking any outside investment. In the process they took a controlled approach to investing in business tools. So, while their company relied heavily on new technology—in particular, the growth and widespread adoption of the Internet—they always used this tool in a manageable and affordable way.

And when it came to spending money on marketing they tried to heed the wisdom spouted by some of their experts. Other companies in this new industry were raising money to use for magazine and television ads; Bourland and Handley focused their marketing on generating great word-of-mouth. When other dot-coms were tapping investors or borrowing money to spend on lavish offices and bloated staff, ClickZ always operated with the minimum of personnel and office space. As a result of their frugal ways, and their good timing, in 2000 the two sold the company, which they founded with an initial investment of essentially nothing—for $16 million.

The point of the story is not that instant riches await those who launch Internet businesses (in fact, the past few years have disproved that myth). The important aspect is that Handley and Bourland were rewarded for becoming masters of one of the primary disciplines for entrepreneurs: *bootstrapping*. They found that once your business becomes operational you must learn to add two and two in order to create five. As stated earlier, a business is a vehicle that *adds value* by delivering a product or service that meets a customer's need. Good entrepreneurs learn to serve their customers through concocting the same value-adding alchemy to their available resources.

Ultimately, bootstrapping is far more than a series of practices that help you save money. Bootstrapping is a way of looking at the world. It's an approach to solving problems, meeting needs, and adding value in the most resourceful and productive manner. Bootstrapping should be the operating philosophy for your business. It's a way of being in the world that enables your company to be as productive at an organizational level as you are at the personal one. This chapter will help you learn to think more creatively about leveraging the resources you have at hand.

Bootstrapping means learning the resourceful skills of Richard Rose, who has grown natural food producer Sharon's Finest into a more than $5 million venture. In his earliest days, Rose would stuff the suggestion boxes of stores who sold his products to convince the

---

"We bootstrapped our company. And I believe that bootstrapping is the best long-term way to grow a business. That's because you aren't relying on money in the bank. You have to learn to be a business. You have to learn to get customers, have to learn smart ways to invest. You have to learn the best way to invest money in your company. If you go into business and overnight you have an advertising and market budget then you just throw it away.

"The reason all these Internet startups failed is because they started out with too much money. In our case we don't have that luxury. So we found effective ways without cash. In marketing, we found that the most bang we got for our buck was word of mouth. We put out small ads in college papers, for example, rather than full page ones in national magazines. There is not one business I have seen on the Internet that has proven to be a viable enterprise."

—Gregg Latterman, Aware Records

owners that legions of customers ached for his products. He created fancy documents on the cheap to convince large-store buyers that his concern was healthy, adding such touches as calling himself "vice-president" to infer that his company was larger than it actually was.

Peter Drucker, one of the great thinkers of the last fifty years, has a simple definition of entrepreneurial activity: "Entrepreneurs, by definition, shift resources from areas of low productivity and yield to areas of higher productivity and yield." You don't have to invent everything anew; you do need to understand how to put the parts together in a new way that creates unique value. This means both seeing the big picture of how your company occupies a distinct niche—and it means developing the more immediate ability of making more of your available resources through innovative management.

In practice, the discipline of bootstrapping has specific applications to how you leverage such resources as your capital, technology, and customer relationships. Here are the key ways in which you'll add value in each.

Seed and Grow Your Company with Minimal Capital

Now, it's critical to distinguish here between being undercapitalized and bootstrapping. Raising capital is a necessary evil for many small businesses. For capital-intensive companies such as a restaurant, say, or a bicycle manufacturer, scurrying for capital is a fact of business life. Moreover, many small companies wither when they cannot take advantage of opportunities because they are limited by fiscal resources. I'm not advocating that you starve your business of necessary fuel.

But I am urging you to reexamine many of the operating assumptions you make about how you can make money and keep going from your available resources. Ask yourself: Is it better to be selling the *idea* of your company to potential investors, or selling *products and services* to actual customers? Chasing capital can be an exhausting and onerous process that can distract us from the business at hand. Chapter 2, "Planning as Learning, Learning as Doing," stressed the importance of using the planning process as a way of getting started rather than getting distracted. The same principle applies to capital. Odds are very high that you can get started with what you have. Always keep an open mind to getting going with your company with the cash you have on hand right now.

And even when you do have a safe capital cushion, you need to spend your money productively. In the business vernacular, *bootstrapping* is another word for frugality. Bootstrap literally refers to the "looped strap sewed at the side or the rear top of a boot to help in pulling it on," or "unaided efforts," but it has come to mean "carried out with minimum resources or advantages." Within a business the term refers to using your available cash and resources in the most resourceful and effective manner. Tom First of Nantucket Nectars says of his early company days, "We paid our bills slowly, collected our receivables as fast as possible, and paid ourselves nothing. That's how you finance a business."

The fact is, most companies have the ability to generate the capital they need for their own growth—even when starting from nothing. Every year *Inc. Magazine* reports on scores of successful companies that were launched with less than $1,000, and grew through generating their own investment capital. By careful cash management, creative financing, and maniacal attention to frugality, each of these bootstrappers could quickly reach critical mass: the point where their cash flow is sufficient to finance their growth. Such an approach is more than a method of cash management. It is a way of life. Taking this route means doing everything from financing your growth through credit cards (if necessary) to operating out of your home to bartering deals with suppliers, to feigning larger size, to much, much more. See the sidebar "Classic Bootstrapping Tips" for a list of specific tips that you can put to immediate use.

As I've said, the value of bootstrapping goes much deeper than merely saving money. Finding ways to squeeze profits and productivity out of your operations enforces frugal behavior that is truly the most powerful lesson in how your business works. Believe it or not, many ostensibly fortunate entrepreneurs rue that they began with too much capital. While it's hard to be too sympathetic to these entrepreneurs, they often learned the hard way that they made poor choices about how to allocate capital and conduct business.

Roxanne Coady certainly learned how the luxury of fallback capital can inadvertently trip up a startup. With more than twenty years' experience as an accountant—and national tax partner—at a Big Eight accounting firm, Coady assumed she had the financial acumen to launch her bookstore R. J. Julia Books in 1990. For the first two years of operation, Coady put her energy into marketing, spending freely on expensive newsletters, glossy packaging, and an excess of staff. She shrugged off the operating losses of her store with the justification that she could afford to subsidize its early growth. Yet when she realized that over the first two years she had lost $233,000 of her own money in the process, Coady realized that the availability of her money allowed her to fantasize that her own business was somehow immune to the rules of the real businesses she used to assist. "As a small business owner, I had acted as if I were somehow exempt from normal financial standards," she says. "Having too much money caused me to think in an unbusinesslike way."

Coady's epiphany—that she needed to train her fiscal discipline on her own business—forced dramatic changes at her store. She began to monitor such details, as whether people needed to print fifty-page reports that weren't useful, and whether she needed to buy such expensive bags for customer purchases. (She didn't.) She began to use cash-flow analysis to monitor how they spent their funds, and whether she needed such a large staff. (She didn't.) She began setting goals with her staff, and asking them to find ways for the store to save— the greatest result being that the store increased its inventory turnover by 50 percent. All these combined efforts helped push her store into the black.

In Chapter 3, "The Numbers That Count," we looked at how to use your critical numbers to find the most profitable activities of your company, and structure your business around these activities. Having this financial insight enables you to spend more time on the activities that generate the most cash for your company. Likewise, bootstrapping should push you toward squeezing the most you can from your available assets. (See the sidebar "One-to-One Marketing.") And, it should encourage you to think creatively about how you might tap new opportunities from your company.

Here are a few immediate practices to take to heart. First, consider pursuing niche markets that you have a better chance of dominating in the early days. Larger competitors will be hesitant to pursue these markets at first, because it will be hard for them to justify their investment. Over time you may ramp up to challenge big companies in big markets, however, in your early days choose your battles wisely. Pursue other products (or even geographic regions) in which you believe that your competition won't jump in and trip you up. Also, be sure to focus on your superior execution and hustle as a means of garnering customers and profits. Over time you may develop a brand, an identity, and perhaps even a technological edge as a means of sustained competitive advantage. All well and good. Such assets can become the basis for sustained excellence and competitive advantage —however, in the beginning, focus on the areas in which you can satisfy customers while making a profit.

Practice "Guerilla marketing"

Guerilla marketing is a phrase invented by author Jay Conrad Levinson that refers to the practice of merging your entrepreneurial spirit with the marketing message you send to customers. By coordinating all your available resources and using them in a manner that exceeds the sum of their parts, you can position your product and company in the marketplace with far greater efficiency than larger companies.

ONE-TO-ONE MARKETING

Consultant-authors Donald Peppers and Martha Rogers have built a very nice consulting business on one simple idea: Rather than spend your time trying to sell your products and services to new customers, focus your time and energy trying to sell more products and services to the same customers. That is, once you've developed a strong relationship, use all your available means to sell more to them. Such an approach forces you to strengthen your conversation with them (that is, keep aware of all their needs) and to find innovative ways to serve them. Staying consistent with their core message, the two have produced a series of books that extends their core message to their core audience: their first, *One-to-One Marketing*, is probably the most useful for applying their ideas.

BOOTSTRAPPING 101

Amar Bhide, the Glaubinger Professor of Business at Columbia University, has studied the practices of scores of successful entrepreneurs. In his 1992 HBR article "Bootstrap Finance," he recommends the following principles and practices:

Get operational quickly. There's nothing ignoble about starting with a copycat idea or product. Big ideas can consume enormous amounts of time and money before they start to generate real money. And being in business can lead you to that breakthrough product you seek.

Look for quick, break-even, cash-generating products. Take baby steps towards blockbuster products (if that's even what you want!) "A business that is making money, elegantly or not, builds credibility in the eyes of suppliers, customers, and employees, as well as self-confidence in the entrepreneur."

Consider high-value products or services that you can sell directly. Convincing customers to give up familiar products or services is very challenging, especially if you don't have a large budget for marketing or advertising. Consider goods that you can sell directly, which lowers costs of sales. Or try to partner up with more established outlets to reach customers (for example, if you are making sweaters, think about persuading a major catalog to carry your products.)

Don't chase high-priced talent. While you need top-notch employees, you probably don't have the means to compensate veterans. Don't settle for lesser-caliber talent—but look instead for diamonds in the rough. Compensate for your startup status by offering advancement and opportunity for growth.

continues

BOOTSTRAPPING 101 (*continued*)

Keep growth in check. Beware new customers whose demands force you to undertake significant new costs. Beware sales that force you to lay out significant money without an unassailable guarantee that you will be made whole. Beware of growth that forces you to add more fiscal strain on your company than you can reasonably expect to meet over time.

Focus on cash, not profits, market share, or anything else. No metrics matter if you can't pay your bills.

Cultivate banks before the business becomes creditworthy. Many banks won't lend to you unless you prove that you merit the loan—which might be difficult without investment capital in the first place. Yet you can place yourself in a position to qualify. Be sure to keep good records, have solid balance sheets, and make a point of making contact with potential bankers, if only to ask for advice. This lays the groundwork for securing a loan down the road.

The first rule is to leverage the resources and assets *that you already control.* Consider the tactics of Catherine Fischer and her partner (and now husband) Kyle Fischer, who are exceptionally skilled at finding innovative ways to stretch their marketing dollars for the Parkway Speakeasy Theater in Oakland. They've exploited the devotion of their loyal community by tapping into Fischer's background in catering and restaurants. "One of the reasons I think the Parkway is successful is that we throw a really good party," she says. A perennial challenge for the theater has been the loss of an audience on nights with big television events such as the Super Bowl or the Oscars. The solution: The Parkway has recaptured their audience by

"Sales is not about you. In fact, when you sell you must place your own needs, ego, and desires in your back pocket. Seems odd, doesn't it. Your own desire to succeed can kill you.

"When you run your own company and when your products and services become entangled in the lives of other people (including employees) you must base desires and vision on those people, not yourself. Once you have learned to always base decisions on the needs and desires of your customers and team members, you find a way to fit them into the rules of your industry and company. It must flow in that direction. The trap that most people fall into is doing this exercise in reverse—and ethics and moral conviction will always lose when company rules and industry rules dictate."

—Tom First, Nantucket Nectars

throwing theme events on those nights. To compete with the Oscar telecast, the Parkway now throws a party that attempts to tap into the excitement of the event. And so patrons are urged, for example, to dress up as if they were going to the Academy Awards, and they receive a glass of champagne while watching the show which is telecast on one of the movie screens.

These and other high-concept, high-profile (yet low-budget) events have given the theater a national profile. When Fischer's sister complained that her infant kept her from going out to the movies, she hatched the idea of a regular Baby Brigade night, in which parents of infants are encouraged to catch up on their nights out by bringing their babies to a special grown-up, infant-friendly showing. This feature (with its cute visual appeal) has garnered national television attention for the business.

Fischer and her partner have also found innovative ways to market to their community. When, in their early days, they found the costs

of placing movie listings in the local newspapers to be too expensive, they launched a monthly newsletter as an alternative. This simple newsletter grew, as a result of positive feedback from their customers, into a twelve-page mailing that included reviews and menus and other nice touches. When it reached a circulation of 4,000, Fischer and her partner found that it had become a victim of its own success—that it had become more expensive than the newspaper listings, and so they had to quit publishing it. Yet it had been a powerful and inexpensive way for them to build on their community. Now, as a means of letting patrons know about future movies and events, they produce a short video commercial on their own and run it before the movies.

Gregg Latterman of Aware Records has also found shrewd ways of spreading the word with limited resources. In order to grow his record company, Latterman has leveraged the work of eight full-time employees with a network of more than 650 nationwide independent reps at colleges and even some in high schools. According to General Manager Mark Cunningham of Aware, the program started in 1994 when a rabid fan named Jason Rio called the company to let them know about his enthusiasm for its compilation CD of unknown bands. Before long he was helping the company informally by putting up posters of the bands around his campus, and even selling the CDs at various fraternity and sorority houses at his college, Michigan State. Latterman quickly turned this passion into a more formal program—initially setting up an 800 number, and then a Web site, for interested fans to become independent representatives for the company.

Since then the success of the program has become self-perpetuating. It has developed such an allure that it draws people who spread the word. Cunningham himself got involved with the company as a representative then an intern, and now works for Aware full-time.

"The independent reps simply want to be a bigger part of the music that they love and want to tell everybody about it," he says. "There are potentially thousands of them around the country. They want to help us and spread the word." They do so by putting up posters for shows and new releases at coffee shops, passing out flyers or stickers or promotional CDs on the street, taking CDs to radio stations or record stores, selling merchandise at concerts, and even picking up bands at the airport (and, for that matter, putting them up at their house if necessary).

"This has all evolved from people simply wanting to help," says Latterman. While managing this far-flung and eclectic network is difficult for the company, Aware certainly benefits disproportionately from the cost, which is next to nothing. The company doesn't pay the reps. Aware does, however, find every way possible to feed the enthusiasm the reps have for the company and the music. "We try to reward them with free music, concert tickets, and a sense of being part of this group of people who love the music that they love," says Cunningham.

Another critical tactic in elevating your passion for your company's core product is elevating your own public profile as a marketing tool. That's what Amy Domini did very deliberately when she launched Domini Social Equity Fund, a socially responsible mutual fund that offered an alternative to traditional investment vehicles in 1990. At the time Domini had no money for advertising or other marketing tactics for the fund, so she relied on her growing expertise in the area as her powerful means of getting the word out. Domini made a point of speaking at every forum possible, from church groups to investment conferences. She also wrote two books on the topic of socially responsible investing—one targeted at individual investors and the other at the investment community.

Domini also worked to cultivate key journalists as a means of reaching a broader audience. She invested in a clipping service to track the subject of socially responsible investing, and made a point of sending every reporter customized material on her work. As a result, she quickly established herself as a trusted source. Moreover, she discovered that the work had a snowball effect—for when new reporters did stories on this topic, they tended to return to the people who had already been quoted in past articles—further leveraging her work.

Domini aimed her sights even higher. When she found that the biggest obstacle to more people signing on was a broadly held belief that socially responsible investing could not compete with the returns of other mutual funds, Domini created a socially responsible index of stocks, tracking the performance of companies that fit her criteria. This index was a marketing coup that simultaneously provided proof that funds such as hers could compete—and became a metric that various financial publications cited frequently, generating more attention for her firm.

Leverage Technology

For small companies, technology represents both a threat and a weapon. The threat lies in two key areas. The first is that technology, especially in the form of new and expensive tools and gadgets, can be expensive, confusing, distracting, and unmanageable for a small, stressed, and already constrained startup. The second threat is that large companies probably have better access to the most recent technology.

The weapon, however, is that large companies are probably no better than you at using technology wisely—and that you have greater flexibility in applying it directly to the mission of your company.

Technology can be bootstrapped as effectively as cash or passion to leverage your resources in the service of customers. The most important question regarding technology and business is this: How does technology help you expand, amplify, or extend the business you've already conceived? In other words, most successful entrepreneurs leverage technology by applying it within a clear business context. Never an end in itself, business tools exist to help you reach your business goals (that is, serving customer needs!) with greater power and efficiency.

Consider Shari Fitzpatrick, whose company Shari's Berries has used the Internet as an inexpensive yet enormously productive channel for finding and serving new customers. Because Fitzpatrick launched her company in 1988, she had years of refining her product of chocolate-dipped strawberries and growing a clientele prior to launching a Web site (**www.berries.com**) in December 1998. Fitzpatrick had grown the company carefully. It took two full years before she moved from her one-bedroom condo to opening her first storefront in 1991, and another three years to open another store. When she launched the Web site in 1998, Fitzpatrick's company had nearly 30 employees and close to $1 million in sales.

By going on the Web she doubled sales in the first year. Fitzpatrick could exploit the Internet so productively because she had already developed a strong community of customers and a well-realized product. The Web site neither interfered with the basic economics of her business nor did it force her to fundamentally rethink her company. It simply exposed her products to a broader customer base.

Even technology startups rarely compete on the technology alone, but on the customer need that they fulfill. This is an important distinction. Consider the company Intuit, which produces the popular Quicken and Quickbooks accounting software. According to founder Scott Cook, the company has always distinguished itself from others in the field through its emphasis on solving consumers' needs simply. "We sell a technology product—but there is a lot of technology out there," says Cook. "We distinguished ourselves by taking the technology and delivering an end product that the customer wanted."

For Intuit, this meant an accounting program that focused very simply on the key financial activities people needed to track. "We built an accounting system without accounting," Cook says, noting that Quicken was designed to avoid the confusion and headaches surrounding traditional accounting software programs, which tended to reflect conventional accounting systems. Quicken was designed as a clear and understandable system based on simple activities such as creating invoices and writing checks. As a result, the company became the market leader within a year of its launch and has remained so to this day.

Even when adding to the product, Intuit always built on the customer's experience. It was one of the first software companies to conduct usability testing, in which it monitored the experience of users and incorporated changes into the product based on what worked or didn't. The company conducted what it called novice testing, in which people with no experience on either the personal computer or with Quicken were observed by Intuit personnel as they installed the program and began to use it. Even today the company continues to focus on the customer experience of this technology-based product. As it has rolled out onto the Web, Intuit has constantly sought ways to recapture the simple user experience in a new medium.

Earlier in this chapter I cited the story of ClickZ as a good example of how a tech company can bootstrap its growth. Virtually every choice that Bourland and Handley made was colored by their lack of startup capital. They paid their Web host in their early days by giving them ad space on their site. They enlisted experts to write for free by concocting what they called queen for a day perks: giving them nice pictures, bios, and links to homepages where these rising stars marketed their services. They grew the company without taking on large investments by working from home for the first year and a half —only renting cheap office space when they had four employees, all working remotely from their homes. (Their first space was 600 square feet located on the second floor of the Andover Anxiety Clinic, a situation that always amused them.) They asked Bourland's brother-in-law, a design student at the time, to produce the logo that defined the company visually.

In terms of technology, they never spent money without a pressing immediate need. Bourland got the site up and running by supplementing his slim technological knowledge with an *HTML for Dummies* book. Handley's first computer, which ran on an IBM 386 chip, didn't even have the computing power to display the Web sites she was providing the copy for! She would have to go over to Bourland's house to see what they were producing. The two chuckle now that one of the first official purchases the company made was a new computer for her.

Ultimately, smart bootstrappers use technology to blur the lines between a small and a large company. That is, technology enables small companies to act big. "The tools now are so good for handling a lot of the basic administrative work that businesses have to do— and hate to do—that it makes it easier for people that have a passion and want to focus on that passion to enter business," says chairman Scott Cook of Intuit. Software programs like Quicken, and its related product Quickbooks (which is designed for small businesses), enable small business owners to grasp the numbers of their business with greater control than before, while a myriad of service providers enable small companies to handle payroll, benefits, and other administrative tasks online. Moreover, most Web-savvy retailers or consultants or anyone with a passion can garner an enormous amount of useful marketing information over the Web—data that was once reserved for large companies.

This doesn't mean, however, that startups are necessarily better suited to use new business tools. Large companies will always have natural advantages over small ones, and the rise, for example, of the Internet has only served to solidify these strengths rather than diminish them. "The most aggressive users and biggest beneficiaries of the web have been big companies," says Scott Cook, who argues that only one company—Amazon—has successfully launched an Internet bookstore (as opposed to many on-line extensions of existing stores). And he notes that the companies with the most established presence on-line are the digital storefronts for successful retailers like L.L. Bean, or major corporations like General Electric.

As this book is written, people are still debating the long-term impact of perhaps the most powerful new business technology for small business: the Internet. My belief is that startups should address the Web as they would any other business tool: as a means to amplify or accelerate the competitive edge they've already developed. The Internet enables you to reach more customers faster, and to make yourself available to existing customers more frequently, and to provide access to your company that was previously logistically challenging. And it helps you get information and connect with customers and vendors. Yet Web proficiency by no means guarantees a successful business. Rather, it's what you do with it.

A FEW CLOSING POINTS

Cultivate Community

Your most valuable asset is the loyalty and commitment of the customer base you create. Your customers form a *community*, and you should take every step possible to recognize and leverage this web of support for your company. There are all types of methods, both formal and informal, for accomplishing this. Roxanne Coady produces a regular newsletter that reviews books, lists upcoming author events at the store, and features a folksy letter from Roxanne. Aware Records formalized its informal bands of boosters into a network of company representatives. And Amy Domini converted the commitment of her customers into future sales by asking them for help in finding new clients. With every monthly shareholder report, Domini would thank them for being customers—and ask them to tell friends about her fund.

Your community can even pitch in with plain old sweat labor. That's how the folks at the Speakeasy Parkway Theater in Oakland used the support of neighbors who wanted to spruce up their part of town. When Fischer and her partner were renovating the theater, which had been dark for more than five years prior to their purchase, they asked members of the neighborhood to come in on the weekend to help with painting and other construction tasks. This secured them hours of cheap labor, and helped build a more loyal band of customers when they opened.

Be Creative in Seeking Help

At this point you've developed business relationships with vendors, customers, partners, and members of your community. Don't be shy in using them. When crunch time comes, you may be able to tap into these relationships for support and resources. That's what Gary Hirshberg did, for example, when his company was faced with a severe cash crunch. When one of his fruit packers couldn't pay Stonyfield Farm, Hirshberg found himself unable, in turn, to pay the company that supplied fruit. So Hirshberg took the advice of a board member who said, "How do you know they will never go for this strategy?" He flew to Ohio to meet with the vendor and confessed that he couldn't pay the $120,000 bill immediately. But he promised he would spend another $160,000 with that vendor over the next six months. And he promised not to buy fruit from anybody else. And he promised to treat the outstanding money as a loan and pay interest on it. Finally, he pledged his personal stock (which was a liability at the time!) as collateral. After mulling it over for a few moments, the vendor agreed to the terms. (Which turned out to be a very good decision for them. Since then Stonyfield has purchased more than $20 million in goods from them.)

Never assume that customers or suppliers are limited to one role. At Toscanini's Ice Cream, owner Gus Rancatore, for example, has converted a number of his loyal customers into investors. And Roxanne Coady cultivated support from all of her early stakeholders. Sales representatives from major publishers, in particular, helped her learn key details about selling books that would have taken her far longer to learn.

Be Ethical!

A word to the wise: Building a company often forces the founder into difficult situations. When it feels like every day, and every decision, is a matter of survival, then one can easily rationalize stretching the truth to employees or vendors, promising something beyond what you can deliver, or outright fibbing to solve a temporary problem. My simple piece of advice: Don't do it. That is, while bootstrapping often involves stretching all your resources—including sometimes, the truth—it stops short of being outright dishonest.

"What I've learned, and what all too many bootstrappers can miss, is that being truthful is good business," says Scott Cook in his famous 1992 essay "The Ethics of Bootstrapping." He continues: "Apart from moral judgements, consider expediency—and expediency is what bootstrapping amounts to. Business is about doing right by the customer and by your business partners, which include vendors and employees. If you do right by them, your business will flourish. If you don't, your business won't. You may solve some temporary bind by fibbing, but it will come back to haunt you. It's not just

---

"While a lot of bootstrapping companies think about *the consequences of failure*—'Gee, if I don't fib about this, I'm going to fail, and if I fail I'll lose all my money, and my wife and kids, and my self-respect'—I don't think they consider the *consequences of success*. What happens if you lie, and are successful? Your customers may know you lied, and employees will definitely know you've lied, and you've set up a culture in which lying's OK—or worse, in which lying is linked with success.

"The things that help make a company successful become the elements of its foundation, the stories through which new employees learn what's right and what's expected of them, and how they can succeed. Do you want those culture legends to be about tricking others? You've got your choice."

Scott Cook, in "The Ethics of Bootstrapping,"
Inc. Magazine, September 1992

---

wrong; it also doesn't work. Being ethical isn't a fairyland, Boy Scout idea, nor is it naïve. I wanted to build a business for the long term. And trust is one of the most important sources of your power."

"A business is a litmus test for how you deal with other things in life," says Tom First, cautioning that hungry entrepreneurs must balance the need to reduce expenses with keeping honest in every sense of the word. When First and Scott launched Nantucket Allserve, he says they felt like they were conducting business under a microscope. Doing business in a tiny island community meant that they couldn't afford to cut corners or act improperly: Simple karma dictated that any false moves would have negative repercussions. "In Nantucket, if you screw one person, you're done," he says. Honest business became an early way of life for them. "When we moved our business off the island and started selling in Boston and Washington, we treated people the same way," says First.

So, at this stage, as your company has become operational, you've learned how you make money and how to operate in the most productive manner. Now's the time when you need to manage the most difficult, and most important, asset of all: other people.

RESOURCES

Honest Business by Michael Philips and Salli Rasberry (Shambala Publishing, Boston, 1996)

This engaging little book tempers a seemingly blind optimism about business as a force for good with great examples of small companies that conduct healthy businesses by following honest principles. It's a given that the book considers honesty a good and moral

TEN CLASSIC BOOTSTRAPPING TIPS

- *Start at home*. There's a reason that fables have grown around the fact that Hewlett-Packard and Apple were founded in garages: because the stories are true. There's nothing ignoble about launching your company from a kitchen table, or working from your living room. When cash got really stretched for Gregg Latterman of Aware Records, he took this move one step further by moving into the company's office for a time.

- *Don't pay yourself.* Imagine how long you can go before your business can pay you a salary—and then add a year. For Gregg Latterman, it took more than six years before he could pay himself a salary comparable to the one he had with Coopers & Lybrand, when he left. And it may take you even longer.

- *Stretch your cash*. Postpone payment and accelerate receivables. Within the boundaries of ethical behavior, be sure to find ways to keep your cash in hand. When it needed cash, Intuit would offer incentives to its customers to pay early.

- *Use the royal "we."* Not to suggest grandeur, but to give the impression always that you are part of a team, part of something larger. Let's put it this way: We suggest it to show the effect this pronoun can have. Potential investors and customers generally prefer to work with established teams rather than just one person. Adopting the plural pronoun is good practice in acting larger.

- *Generate word-of-mouth*! Good word-of-mouth is not only priceless but it is also possible to create cheaply. Turn your friends and family into company zealots. Call talk shows. Post on chat boards. Stuff suggestion boxes in stores. Post flyers. Write letters to the editor. Take twelve other actions that start people talking about your company. Repeat.

continues

TEN CLASSIC BOOTSTRAPPING TIPS *(continued)*

- *Master your laptop.* Tap into your computer, the Internet, voice mail, and other tools to leverage your individual effectiveness.

- *Haggle.* Never routinely accept a fixed price. Asking vendors for favorable discounts became second nature to Laura Peck Fennema when building Essentiel Elements. "If you don't ask for it you don't get it," she says. Despite buying in small lots, her company would often receive price breaks on bottles, labels, or boxes, because she persuaded the vendors that her company would one day buy in sufficient volume to merit a volume price. And partly as a result of the savings she squeezed out, her promise came true.

- *Exploit cheap labor.* Okay, not exploit in the sense of exploitive, but more like resourceful and shrewd redirection of other people's natural energies. (All right—read "be ethical" for guidance here.) Are there local college students who would do an internship with you? Local teenagers, friends, and family, who are willing to pitch in with low-end activities to help you out? What does your business offer to reward loyal supporters in a frugal though meaningful way?

- *Ask*! Try these phrases: "May I pay you in sixty days instead of thirty?" "Can you give me a price break on that supply?" "Would you be willing to let me try this piece of equipment out as a demo for the first three months?" "How do you feel about barter?" "No, don't put that check in the mail—I'll come pick it up." "May I come speak to your church group/rotary club/Elks convention/[fill in the blanks]?"

- *Turn customers into your sales force.* Convert their passion into your company's success. Ann Marie Stanton found many new customers through the passion of one early client, who was so loyal that she held regular luncheons for Stanton to show her wares.

quality for a business. The book goes much further, however, by explaining how this code becomes an operating set of rules for running a meaningful business.

Guerilla Marketing by Jay Conrad Levinson (Houghton Mifflin, New York, 1993)

Levinson coined the phrase Guerilla Marketing and did a brilliant job of building it into a brand, a series of books that detail a bootstrapped approach to marketing, finance, selling, and more. The flagship book, *Guerilla Marketing*, takes an extremely broad approach. It considers marketing to comprise just about every choice you make in producing your product and getting it in the hands of customers, from conceiving and naming the product to manufacturing it and then getting the word out. Within this framework Levinson offers countless ideas and suggestions for cheaply and effectively cultivating and serving regular customers.

Bootstrapping packages from *Inc. Magazine*

You want great stories and lively tips on leveraging your spirit and resources? Check out the annual bootstrapping packages from *Inc. Magazine*, whose annual roundup of great companies started with less than $1,000 is an inspiration and a recurrent tutorial on how small companies can perform alchemy. (Go to the Web site **www.inc.com** and search for "bootstrapping.") The package is a vivid reminder that most companies get started with a minimum of capital and a maximum of ingenuity and hustle. And it provides proof that even billion-dollar companies can be formed with literally nothing down.

A Goal is a Dream with a Deadline by Leo Helzel and Friends (McGraw-Hill, New York, 1995)

This short, quirky book of aphorisms could easily fit into just about any chapter as a resource. Yet since Helzel structures his thirty-plus years of insight about starting a company as a series of short aphorisms on how to think and act like an entrepreneur, I like to think of it as a guide to the bootstrapping mentality. A couple of my favorites: "The difference between women and men entrepreneurs is gender," and "Entrepreneurship is like parenting. If you wait until everything is right, you'll never get started."

Working Solo by Terri Lonier (Wiley, New York, 1994)

Another great collection of strategies for making the most of what you have. This book focuses on the single entrepreneur, a distinction that is particularly useful in devising ways for you to increase your own productivity and effectiveness. Lonier is also particularly good at addressing the personal issues you confront not only in boot-strapping but also simply as a company founder.

The 7 Habits of Highly Effective People by Steven Covey (Fireside, New York, 1989); and *The Effective Executive* by Peter F. Drucker (Harper, New York, 1985)

Some may find Covey's lessons for becoming more effective too abstract and moral for their taste (at times I confess to be one of them). Yet the value of this book outweighs such a criticism. Your personal productivity is at the heart of your organization. Your ability to lever-age your personal energy pays off both directly (in how you leverage the organizational capacity) and indirectly (in how you model effective behavior to employees and other community members). Covey's lessons may be treacly, but they work

While Drucker's contribution skews toward executives in larger organizations, he still provides crystalline insights into how individuals in any organization can leverage their efforts dramatically. Best of all, unlike other guides for personal effectiveness, Drucker tailors his advice to one's behavior as the leader of an organization. Effective executives do the following: know where their time goes, gear their efforts to results rather than to work, build on strengths, concentrate on the key areas leading to outstanding results, and make effective decisions.

5

Walking the Line

LEARN TO MANAGE RELATIONSHIPS WITH CLARITY BY SETTING BOUNDARIES, ESTABLISHING MUTUAL EXPECTATIONS, AND ENFORCING CONSEQUENCES

"Employees are the source of the biggest frustrations in this business," says Gus Rancatore of Toscanini's Ice Cream. What's so hard? "Getting people to do what you want them to do. Getting them to do what is best for the business," he says. And then there's dealing with rude or belligerent employees. There's the hassle of paperwork, the nuisance of employees thrusting their personal problems on him, and even the underlying threat of lawsuits. Rancatore has to constantly work with the psychic weight of feeling responsible, in one form or another, for the needs and satisfaction of his employees.

On the other hand, says Rancatore, his workers are also the source of the greatest joy in his business. "You work with people and you marvel how you learn from your employees as they make little and big suggestions," he says, adding, "You see how they grow." Rancatore, whose stores are sprinkled in both urban settings and on campus at the Massachusetts Institute of Technology (MIT), has a clientele and an employee base that reflect a wide diversity. Some of his employees come with minimal job skills, while others are literally rocket scientists. He's learned from them all. "The MIT students have taught me about hard work and organization," says Rancatore. In fact, over the years he has learned more about subjects as diverse as material sciences to rowing to the culture of hardcore music to Reynaud's scattering syndrome than he could have ever imagined. Moreover, Rancatore has had the satisfaction of training employees who have gone on to careers in the food industry.

Rancatore's struggles—and celebrations—reflect a common experience among entrepreneurs. That's because managing people is one of the most difficult challenges in starting a company. The earliest days of startups are often characterized by a complete lack of boundaries—and not merely between your company and yourself. The lines between work and family, between friends and coworkers, between sense of self and sense of company worth—all tend to blur under the pressure of getting a business up and running. It becomes easy to confuse the work life with all of life, and to use the workplace as an environment for airing personal matters that are often better addressed outside the office.

This lack of boundaries can make it painfully difficult to manage others—because you are often challenged not so much by the personality and emotions of others, but by your own quirks and

"People were a lot harder than I expected. They were more dishonest, angrier, and more cut-throat in many cases. When things came down to money, it always seemed like people were total phonies—they would say anything to get what they want. Tommy and I tried to continue to 'be who we were' even when lawyers would tell us to act a certain way. It never really burned us either—but business is pretty cut-throat and people are often out for themselves. By the same token, the good people in business are nicer and more honest than you could ever hope for or expect. We ran into a few of those types and they would make you believe in the world all over again."

—Tom First, Nantucket Nectars

deeply buried emotions. It's bad enough that your company is a vehicle that tests the validation and excitement you need at some level, but when you mix in the human dynamic of needing other employees to help you with this mission, you have created a potentially explosive situation. Your psychic needs will almost certainly differ radically from your employees'—which is not such a bad thing. Your challenge, however, is to learn to be aware of how your needs differ from your employees', and then use these different skills, aspirations, and goals to manage the organization in the most effective and productive manner.

"The job of a professional manager is not to like people. It is not to change people. It is to put their strengths to work," says Peter Drucker. This calls for a delicate balance on your part—in which you tread the line between formal systems and policies that enable people to get work done routinely and in a standard manner, while retaining the personal spirit and flexibility that allow individuals to thrive.

In a small business, the most difficult dynamic in managing others effectively is the lack of boundaries that necessarily accompany a startup. Learning how to get the most out of people and yourself rests on your ability to play both manager and leader, to celebrate the human element of your company while ensuring that work gets done in the most effective manner.

That's why the key to managing effectively rests in your learning to set boundaries. Boundaries, in the form of explicit policies, clear communications, respect for others' personal space, and the mutual establishment of goals and expectations, form a productive context in which you and your employees can get great things done. These boundaries create an explicit standard by which you and your employees can track progress. These boundaries help create an impersonal set of standards in what may otherwise feel like an intensely personal realm.

This chapter will help you set and walk these boundaries. We'll look at how to make your expectations explicit for yourself and for others, how to motivate others through your own personal conduct, and, most importantly, how to navigate the emotional gray area that can easily trip up a small group of people who are trying to work together.

"I found the HR thing to be the most difficult area—the one that almost ruined my business. I was so bad at managing people. I had no boundaries. I did things with people that would make your hair stand on end. And now I see it so differently. I see that you can create a structure so that there are boundaries. It's almost like raising children."

—Lori Duke, *Woman Magazine*

Becoming the boss of others is not an easy step to take. Far too many small company owners are too concerned with whether their employees like them or not. Owner Roxanne Coady of R. J. Julia Books just wanted her staff to like her in the early days. "I wanted them as my friends," she says. But she learned the hard way that this is a recipe for failure. "I found out the hard way that I had basically reinvented a dysfunctional family," she says. Coady knew so much personal information about some employees that she sometimes thought twice about imposing work pressure on them, and in some cases shied away from conducting performance reviews. She avoided keeping people accountable for their commitments. Coady eventually came to realize that the point is not to be liked, but to create healthy conditions in which her employees can find their own meaningful work.

Choose Your Culture

Another word for the set of boundaries that describe how your employees work together is *culture*. Culture means much more than a tacit consensus about acceptable clothes to wear and how people should blow off steam. Culture cuts to the core of how people get along, how they work, and how you organize, motivate, and "control" them. Culture refers to the values, beliefs, and attitudes of an organization. As founder of the company, one of your key decisions is to deliberately choose the type of culture you'll have—specifically, what kind of philosophy will inform the way you manage your employees.

One of the most influential (though not best-known) thinkers in the field of organizational behavior in the last century is a former MIT

professor named Douglas McGregor, whose 1960 book *The Human Side of Enterprise* helped pioneer a new approach to management. McGregor came up with a powerful insight that applies to those who organize others to work in pursuit of a common goal. All managers operate out of implicit theories about why people work. "At the core of any theory of the management of human resources are assumptions about human motivation," he wrote. You may not have thought about these beliefs consciously, says McGregor, yet they nonetheless inform virtually every decision you make when dealing with employees.

McGregor separated people's mental models into two divergent camps, which he labeled Theory X and Theory Y. Theory X, which McGregor found to be the more traditional view of direction and control, holds that most people don't like work and will avoid it if possible. They have little ambition, seek security, and prefer to be directed by others. Therefore, effective managers have to coerce and control them. They can only achieve organizational goals with such people by threatening them with punishment or bribing them with treats and rewards.

On the other hand, McGregor conceived Theory Y, which he believed reflected an entirely different theory of human motivation. In Theory Y, individuals see work as a potentially satisfying endeavor, an activity in which they can earn responsibility and exercise self-control. Under the right conditions, individuals in Theory Y develop personal goals that line up with their organizations and bring more satisfaction to both. Such a system believes in the capacity of individuals to learn and thrive, and calls for a different set of choices for managers. Their role is to create the conditions that enable individuals to integrate their goals with the company, and to then find the right form of "control" for each individual, enabling them to learn, grow, and produce to their highest potential.

There's a point to this academic digression. I'm not advocating that one type of culture is best for all organizations. Some companies thrive with a militaristic command-and-control structure, while others are more effective with a progressive setup, in which the collective group of employees has great independence and a say in how decisions are made. Most companies, in fact, fall somewhere in between. It's impossible to say which form is best suited for you. But I can say that *you must choose one*. Your organization, and the way you manage your employees, will reflect fundamental beliefs about whether people can make their own decisions, come up with their own goals, and work with the initiative to find ways to integrate these goals with those of the company. Your policies should be consistent with these beliefs because the worst form of management is one that says one thing and does another—or that believes one thing and practices another. It's far more effective, smarter, and, well, less painful to make these beliefs explicit up front instead of discovering them in retrospect.

"The success of any form of social influence or control depends ultimately upon altering the ability of others to achieve their goals or satisfy their needs," says McGregor. Therefore, the role of the manager is to find the style that fits most appropriately for the nature of work in your company, the culture you have designed, and the goals and makeup of your employees.

Granted, many questions about the type of culture you will have, the manner in which you manage employees, the style of decision-making, and the specific policies in everything ranging from maternity leave to equity-sharing to brand identity are determined on a

"A fallacy is often revealed in managerial attempts to control human behavior. When we fail to achieve the results we desire, we tend to seek the cause everywhere but where it usually lies: in our choice of inappropriate methods of control. The engineer does not blame water for flowing downhill rather than up, nor gases for expanding rather than contracting when heated. However, when people respond to managerial decisions in undesired ways, the normal response is to blame them. It is *their* stupidity, or their uncooperativeness, or their laziness which is seized on as the explanation of what happened, not management's failure to select appropriate means for control . . . .

"We can improve our ability to control only if we recognize that control consists in selective adaptation to human nature rather than in attempting to make human nature conform to our wishes."
—Douglas McGregor, *The Human Side of Enterprise*, pp. 10-11

case-by-case basis. Yet having a clear statement or idea of values and beliefs enables these decisions to be made with far greater clarity and purpose. (See the sidebar "What Does Your Company Stand for?)

And don't forget the importance of a mission as motivator. "There's no question that the existence of a clear mission statement proved to be one of the most powerful attractants to the talents that I needed," says CEO Gary Hirshberg of Stonyfield Farm. Hirshberg says the mission of being profitable, while seeking ways to be environmentally responsible, helped not so much for what it literally said, but what it represented to others. "The key early hires were not ecofacists like me. But the fact that I was willing to say that this is important told them that this was an interesting place, a human place." Many of Hirshberg's early hires were what he called high-tech refugees,

---

WHAT DOES YOUR COMPANY STAND FOR?

As you begin to formally analyze how your company will deliver on the promise you envision, it should be getting clear that you are creating one profound product: *your company itself.* This distinction may not feel significant, especially if you are running a one- or two-person company. If you start doing business with core values and beliefs that determine how you deal with customers, employees, and community, you must make a conscious and deliberate effort to manifest these beliefs. Otherwise, you will find yourself with policies and procedures that don't necessarily match the business you want, nor will they prove to be particularly effective.

In his best-selling book *Built to Last*, Jim Collins argues the importance of identifying your company's core values. "Core values are the organization's essential and enduring tenets—a small set of timeless guiding principles that require no external justification; they have *intrinsic* value and importance to those inside the organization," he says. For Procter and Gamble, it has been product excellence; at Nordstrom, a core value is subservience to the customer.

So, you must constantly ask what the core values of the company—and of yourself—are. How do you translate these beliefs into products and policies? And how do you express these values to the employees who comprise your company?

---

employees who were burned out with corporate life and sought a company that respected both the bottom line and a broader goal—in this case, that of being environmentally responsible. "People wanted a place where their human needs—including the need to take time off to coach a softball game—were revered."

Finding the Right Employees

There's an easy solution, of course, to building the perfect culture with the perfect workforce: hire perfect employees from the outset and then just sit back while they run the show.

Yeah, right. Actually, the real-world equivalent to this dream is to hire the *right* people for your organization. When sizing up candidates for your company, you need to consider how they fit with your company culture. Ask yourself how well their individual skills and experience match up with company needs. This means both listening to your gut about whether you like them or not *and* developing a screening process for matching the candidates' assets to your organization's needs. Your primary consideration, especially with early candidates who will have new responsibilities as your company grows, is how well their personal mission and skills line up with what you believe your company will accomplish. Will this individual's strengths and weaknesses change the mix you and others bring to the table in a positive way?

Bear in mind that the highest form of leverage you can achieve when hiring people is to hire the *right* people. "It's not how you man-

---

"When I was starting out I believed that other people were important, but that the success of the company was seventy percent due to the entrepreneur and thirty percent due to the other people. Over time I have come to flip that percent. Now I believe that at the end of the day it is the people that you surround yourself with that relates more to the success of the venture than to the individual entrepreneur. So hopefully what the entrepreneur is doing is picking the right people."

—Martin Babinec, Trinet

---

age people, but who you manage in the first place," says Jim Collins. That's why the Marines, who are famed for their organizational prowess, are reported to tap their best soldiers for recruiting. In a startup, you have little room for error. Your managerial time must be spent on, for lack of a better word, the "right things." You cannot afford the agony and misery of trying to manage unmanageable employees. I'm not talking simply about the thieves and rebels who are clearly wrong for any company, but even the unmotivated and grumpy ones that aren't helping your company move forward. One of the more painful lessons to learn in hindsight is this: you will spend much more time and generate far more negative emotions trying to mine poor employees than you will with your good ones. This isn't simply an issue of psychic health and emotional well-being, but managerial efficiency. Excellent employees don't simply produce more for the company: they release you to be more productive as well. So, hire the right people, and have the courage and discipline to dispatch those who aren't making the grade. Pruning your workforce early will save you pain and suffering and create the opportunity to bring the *right* employees on the bus.

You have many mechanisms, both formal and informal, for gauging a potential employee's fit with your company. The challenge, of course, is choosing one that feels consistent with your company's culture. Founder Marion McGovern of M Squared has become a huge proponent of the quick *Predictive Indicator* (PI) test as a means of determining how a candidate will fit. This diagnostic simply matches the personality of the individual to the demands of the prospective position.

Amy's Ice Cream in Austin, Texas, has become famous for a very different method of gauging the right employees. The company values fun and wants employees to enjoy themselves in the process of spreading good cheer to customers. So, as a symbolic gesture of encouraging workers to have fun and be creative, Miller uses a white paper bag as the application form. Yes, a simple white paper bag. Candidates are asked to do anything they want with the bag and to bring it back in a week. Those who simply write their name and address on the bag often fail to make the cut. Those who get a job have done everything from create elaborate works of art to humorous speeches to even a jack-in-the-box scooper. Many of these successful applications now hang on the walls of the company's stores, sending a further message to Amy's community of what the company stands for.

Founder Gregg Latterman of Aware Records certainly believes that the trick to developing the right culture is to spend far more time making sure to hire the right people than on training them the right way. "I started at a big company and my theory was to not set boundaries and to let people live the way they wanted to," he says of launching a company. Thus, Aware has, for example, no set amount of allotted vacation days. "If people want to take a day off, they just take a day off," Latterman explains. This hands-off philosophy clicked for Aware only after Latterman had staffed the company with employees who could optimize their personal output under these rules. "It's more about finding the right people than setting the right boundaries," he learned. "Most people want boundaries. They want a schedule and want to be told what to do. And those are not the people I want here. I have people who are self-starters. We are a small company and we evolve and everybody has to be very smart and political." (See the sidebar "Hiring Smart.")

HIRING SMART

"When you hire your first employees, every single hire has huge implications for the success or failure of the company," says Martin Babinec. "When you are at a hundred people and make a bad hire it's not such a big deal. When you are at two employees and make a bad hire, it can kill your business."

Although hiring smart is an acquired trait, here are some tactics to help ensure that you bring on the right people from the start.

Check references! Some entrepreneurs find this process uncomfortable or unwieldy. Get used to it. It's a vital step in testing whether your gut reaction is correct about a candidate.

Hire according to where the company is going. "If the early hires are going to be keepers, then the most important attribute for them is the ability to evolve and grow as the business grows," says Babinec.

Ask what the candidate believes. The most important fit is that of values and beliefs. Skills and experience count for a lot and should be part of the equation, but they can be taught or developed.

Put teeth into the tryout period. Make every human effort to ensure the success of every hire. But don't prolong the mutual torture of a candidate who isn't working out. Spend extra time in the probationary period to ensure that this match will work for both of you.

Establish Shared Goals and Mutual Expectations

Simply having the right employees isn't enough for success. You must also find mechanisms that enable people to thrive. The most powerful is the establishment of mutual goals and expectations. Such

a practice becomes an external and explicit standard by which you and your workers can gauge how well they are doing.

When owner Roxanne Coady of R. J. Julia Books took a more professional approach toward her staff, one of the first moves she made was to establish individual goals that were integrated with the store's mission. When launching the bookstores, Coady had struggled to get the most out of her employees and was constantly frustrated. One key reason: she operated out of an implicit belief that her employees shared her commitment and goals for the store, while, of course, they had their own personal reasons for being there and sources of satisfaction that were at times entirely different from hers. She had been running at such a pace, however, that she simply expected others to be like her. "I tended to talk only about what I needed to get done," says Coady.

Such an attitude kept her from acknowledging the pressures of others. Taking a step back, however, and adapting a more professional approach toward managing people led her to help each employee develop an individual set of goals. Coady then began meeting with them regularly to help track their progress.

Depending on the type of culture you choose, you can make the goals and expectations as rigid or as loose as needed. Some employees may find the pressure of rigid targets demoralizing or stressful, while others thrive under competitive settings that celebrate winners and losers. The challenge, again, is finding the right mechanisms for your company—and then lining them up with the company's mission.

Finally, be sure to help employees *excel at what they are good at.* "Workers want to know the rules and the limits, but you still have to be flexible," says Gus Rancatore. This means sometimes accommodating the quirks of certain workers in order to reap the benefits of their unique skills. One Toscanini's scooper, for example, was per-haps the fastest and most people-oriented ever—yet compensated for these skills by being "the human incarnation of the Peanuts charac-ter Pigpen." Although he could wait on 200 customers in an hour and keep them happy, at the end of that time the store would resemble a frat house after a beer blast. Rancatore ultimately learned to maximize the contribution of this employee by teaming him up with coworkers who had an exaggerated sense of cleanliness and order.

Communicate!

Good managers maintain an active culture by letting everyone in the company know what's going on in both little and big matters. Developing good communications by everyone is the key to coordi-nating the work of you and your employees. This practice, however, can be very easy to forget. Entrepreneurs are often so busy with the mad rush of company details that they forget that constant commu-nication can be the most effective form of management. Good and regular communications help employees match their work to the needs of the company, bolster morale, and keep the spirit of what fuels the company alive.

Communication, of course, comes in many forms. When you have few employees, it may take the form of quick, frequent talks or constant emails updating current situations or demands. Many com-panies try to hold Friday lunches, or other informal meetings, on a regular basis to discuss current company events. Or, you may want to schedule a more formal weekly meeting to share key information.

One great tool is a short, regular written note to your employ-ees. One great example of this is practiced at Toscanini's Ice Cream. Every night Gus Rancatore writes a recap of the day's activities and hangs this letter on a clipboard on the wall where employees can read it. These missives, which collectively form a diary of the company's soul, contain the day's numbers, recount each store's daily financial performance, share funny stories about employee heroics and travails, and mention any new relevant company information. They serve as a great way to celebrate the store's culture and to keep individuals focused on the important matters at hand.

As M Squared grew, McGovern began to feel less connected to her employees. In the early days she knew everyone's name and their family life, but as the company grew and opened far-flung offices, that relationship became impossible. McGovern worried that as a result the manifestations of the values of the company were no longer obvious, so she set out to find a means of connecting people to that history. Almost like having stories for children, McGovern instituted a way to keep the company values alive. She began writing a weekly email and sent it to everyone in the company. These electronic letters did far more than simply share news of new clients, celebrate great work by employees, or talk about company events. McGovern also used them to keep her employees aware of the broader company mission. (See the sidebar "Leading by Storytelling.")

Ultimately, it doesn't matter what precise form your communications take. It just matters that you let your employees know what they need to know.

Foster the Spirit of Accountability

Regardless of the choices you make about culture, communication, or individual hires, your startup must live by one key quality: accountability. Just as your company must deliver on every promise it makes to customers (or give a clear explanation as to why it fails to in extra-

LEADING BY STORYTELLING

Great communications motivate employees by periodically reminding them of why they're working for the company in the first place. Here's a nice example by Marion McGovern to her M Squared employees, rallying the troops:

"Permit me a departure from my regular update, even though it was a busy week of training, CBI strategy formulation, high touch committee recommendations, etc. Not to worry, I'll keep you posted next week. Perhaps this message would have been better suited on July 4th, but nonetheless, please allow me a little poetic license . . .

"On this date back in 1789, the French common folk stormed the Bastille Prison in Paris and freed all its prisoners (mostly political ones), eventually reducing the hated symbol of tyranny to rubble. (Although many years ago, my husband and I did look for it in Paris—I was a German major after all . . .) The fact is that there were only a few prisoners left in the prison at that time, but such details never bother the French when they get excited and take to the streets. Speaking of which, the alley behind our headquarters here will be hopping tonight!

"M Squared also has an independent streak, and this is an appropriate day to remind ourselves of one of our most cherished company values: EMPOWERING INDEPENDENCE. In our 'M Squared Values Statement' we characterize 'Our Core Purpose' as such:

'To invigorate the management workforce by empowering independent talent.'

"Our intent in framing that phrase was to include not only our consultants in the 'independent talent' category, but also our clients and

continues

ourselves. We give our clients the freedom to secure a great consultant to handle an urgent task.

"For ourselves, our mode is to hire great people and give them the freedom (as well as support) to do their best and achieve wonderful things for the company, while having the independence to pursue a balanced life for themselves. This independence is the very essence of our culture.

"Moreover, we have helped hundreds (maybe thousands?) of independent consultants improve their professional opportunities and, by extension, their personal lives, and it is our fervent hope that we may continue to bring the power of the independent workplace to help many more consultants and clients in California and New England, and next year other cities as well (I'll keep you on the edge of your seat here . . .) and eventually throughout the world. (Yes, we are talking about an M Squared empire . . . where's my tiara?) More importantly, we will have fun doing it too, thanks to the value we put as a company on independence . . .

"So please join me today in a virtual toast (either with French bubbly or your choice of other libation) to the independence of M Squared, the French and people everywhere—as the song goes, "People everywhere just got to be free . . ." (Was that the Young Rascals?)

"Have a wonderful day and weekend."

ordinary situations,) so too must employees do what they say they will. Just as, for that matter, you must model this value by always following through on your commitments. I mention this quality because many company founders, especially those who are new to managing people, discover that they have to deal with the messy side of managing people, such as having to confront employees who don't do what they say they will do or don't do what they need to do.

As the leader of the company, you have to be prepared to deal with people when they fail to follow through on agreed goals. "People need to know what the rules are, and that if they break them there are consequences," says Lori Duke, who has learned that employees must be accountable for what they say they'll do. Perhaps the toughest managerial task for new entrepreneurs is establishing consequences when people fail, over time, to get their work done. In the best of systems, you have hired the right person, established healthy goals that are beneficial for the individual and the company, and have a great two-way communication system in place that supports the work and discovers obstacles to people's progress. Even in these small company utopias, there will be employees who just don't get the job done, which puts you in the uncomfortable role of the heavy.

Just as the broader challenge of managing people is to establish impersonal rules and policies, the trick to enforcing consequences rests in keeping matters focused on results, promises, and other data —as opposed to veering into hard emotional assessments. Even so, most entrepreneurs find the emotional demands of making employees accountable to be brutal.

"Entrepreneurs are very afraid of their employees leaving," says Lori Duke. "You feel that you will never exist without them, so you never measure them in a professional way." Most entrepreneurs find that firing their first employee is one of the most painful, excruciating decisions that they one day look back on and recognize they had to do. When she was building a publishing company, for example, Duke would hold on to employees long after she knew they had to go. She would excuse their shortcomings and avoid confrontations when people failed to do what they said they would. In so doing she simply exacerbated the situation. All because in her small company, comprised mostly of women, Duke put a premium on being liked—which she somehow believed would change if she fired someone. Only after she sold the company to a larger company, while retaining daily control, did Duke learn to become more dispassionate about accountability.

Laura Peck Fennema also remembers the "personal anguish" of letting go her first employee. "It's harmful to have to let someone go when they are a wonderful person but can't do what they need to do," she says. Fennema came to this painful decision with one of her first employees who simply couldn't keep pace as the company grew. Although other employees learned to accept more responsibility, this individual continued to rely on others, and Fennema finally concluded that she had to go. These decisions, even when correct, don't come easily. It took a full two years for Gregg Latterman to finally let one early employee go, a time during which he unintentionally prolonged his agony.

FORMAL BOUNDARIES AREN'T ALWAYS STRONG ENOUGH

Of course, situations will occur, especially in startups, where you enlist friends and family, where boundaries aren't sufficient to ensure rational behavior among workers. That's because stronger forces may be at play—the power of preexisting relationships. Times will arise when you have to recognize that, company boundaries or not, some prior relationships have a power that a business can't erase. Many entrepreneurs who found companies with friends and family find that, regardless of their efforts to create new rules, old roles prevail. (Also, they often find that wishing that external relationships will completely adapt to their new roles isn't enough. See the sidebar "Can You Balance Work and Family?")

CAN YOU BALANCE WORK AND FAMILY?

In short, no. The word *balance* is probably a misnomer when applied to the conflict between raising a family, especially with young children, and starting a company. Yes, it's possible to have both—but I have found in most cases that entrepreneurs find that either one or the other suffers, and that both compete rather than complement one another. This may sound fairly self-evident—yet it is also a rather difficult issue for many entrepreneurs to recognize and acknowledge. Here's a dirty little secret: it's much easier to start a company and family simultaneously if you have someone else raising the family. Don't shy away from this truth. Let me be absolutely clear here: I'm not advocating a return to one parent working 60 hours and the other devoting one's full life to the kids. But I feel strongly that you need to be honest with yourself and your partner about the time, effort, and mental commitment that a startup demands.

WANT TO TEAM UP?

Should you choose a partner in your venture? The pros are many: a partner can bring resources, experience, contacts, and skills to the table. A partner provides companionship and a reality check in the grueling entrepreneurial journey. It's great to have a comrade to bounce ideas off of,

continues

WANT TO TEAM UP? (*continued*)

to keep you mired in reality, and to share the ups and downs of your journey. Having a team, whether two or more, can help you feel more confident and powerful in your quest.

And yet certainly downsides exist as well. That biggest risk is that taking on a partner means exposing yourself to the quirks and foibles of another person. Unless you have utter faith in your partner's abilities, you are taking a blind leap of faith that they can help you realize the company you envision. The freedom and control you've gained in establishing your own business are immediately mitigated by the fact that you must share decisions and control with another individual. Emotionally, you are tied to this person in a bond that may feel tighter than marriage.

For these reasons, you should weigh heavily the decision of whether to partner up. And if you should decide to move forward, I would suggest but one cardinal rule: choose someone with compatible values. It's a good thing to bring on a partner with complementary skills. If you are great at selling the vision but aren't as versed in the nitty-gritty of making it work, for example, your team will be considerably improved by someone with a flair for operations. As I said, that's good. But what's *fundamental* is this: you must line up with someone whose values are aligned with yours. Otherwise, when it comes to critical decisions that speak to the core of your company, you may encounter destructive and irreconcilable differences. So, if you should take on a partner, walk through a series of questions that test how well your core values are aligned with one another.

When Jeffrey Mount bought Wright's Gourmet House, his grandparents' restaurant business in Tampa, Florida, he decided to bring in his sister as a partner. Her skills in the kitchen complemented his talents as manager of the enterprise. He didn't plan, however, on their history of being siblings to dominate the tenor of their business relationship. Because he "confused family preferences with good business practices," Mount made several key decisions based purely on emotional reasons rather than on good business sense. Jeff wanted to pour the company's cash flow back into the business, with the goal of expanding aggressively. Yet his sister, seeking more of a livelihood from a predictable source, fought for a more conservative, immediately lucrative approach. The cost to the business was an acrimonious battle at the top that paralyzed both of them and demoralized others.

Only when Mount began seeking the outside counsel of professionals when making major decisions did he begin making decisions for the good of the business and not the family. Eventually, he forced his sister out and took control of the restaurant. Although it took time for them to heal their personal rift, they did come to recognize how their business battle recapitulated many of their childhood struggles. And the business itself grew once their in-fighting was removed.

Mount learned the hard way that old relationships—especially family ties—often prevail over the ties that should bind within a company. As Mount learned, "Family members break the rules of business because we're family, and then we're horrified when we suffer the consequences of our reckless behavior."

I like to think of the Gerace brothers, Sam and Tom, as good examples of finding the right tension in their work relationship. When he was growing up, Tom would rarely catch the attention of Sam, who was eight years older and who would include his kid brother only when his friends needed a prop to disappear in their magic act. Yet both brothers remember something that Sam said to Tom when he was about 15. By then, Tom had enough clout to bother Sam when he needed attention—and had outgrown the time when Sam's idea of fun was letting Tom help in the magic act. At the time, Tom remembers, Sam told him that the two of them could have a lot more fun doing things if they both worked on things from their own angle. If they wanted to build a tree fort, for example, it would go smoother if they each did what they could—instead of Sam building it and Tom tearing it down.

This candid assessment of their relative strengths helped the two when they launched Be Free in 1996, a company that helps others market on the Internet. Both brothers say they adopted this "tree fort principle" to their relationship as cofounders of the company. Each took a distinctly different role with the company, suited to his strengths and background. The two set a policy of always talking through any conflicts—with the prior agreement that "we would stop doing business together if we ever found we could not be honest with one another," says Sam. Today, despite suffering a bit at the hands of the Internet slowdown, the two remain in business together. "I think even today our company culture has evolved out of how Sam and I handle our relationship," says Tom. "We manage very openly."

To Manage Others, Manage Yourself

The Gerace brothers' relationship is a nice reminder that you manage others by managing yourself. It's one thing to say you will set standards, have good communication, and patiently empower others to get things done in your new company. It's an entirely different matter to follow through on these matters. Asking others to set goals and get things done requires a consistency, clarity, and openness on your part that is difficult in a startup. Company founders tend to have a passion for the product and an excitement about realizing great things that make it difficult for them to accept more modest goals and less-intimate product knowledge of their employees. Moreover, the constant pressures of a startup allow one to constantly excuse or justify behavior that alienates, discourages, and even hinders employees. It's particularly difficult to see how one's behavior—even the parts you may consider your strengths—can hinder others from doing their job well.

That's why it's important to remember that managing others will always be an intensely personal task, and that you shouldn't ignore what's going on inside of you as you give orders. Just as your business reflects a set of personal goals and values, so does your managerial style emanate from your individual values, passions, purpose, and identity. You can't guide others without making some of these abstract forces concrete. This doesn't mean regaling coworkers with sob stories of your upbringing or sharing your emotions at every opportunity. But it does mean acknowledging the basis for your decisions, and letting others know that your decisions stem from a personal viewpoint.

"Often with the entrepreneur, the qualities that drive them to be an entrepreneur aren't the ones driven to create a conducive environment for a team to succeed. The entrepreneur is so I-focused and driven, and their identity and vision are so intimately intertwined. Those skills don't always lend themselves to asking, how are we going to build a team to do that?"

—Kevin Cashman

"Authenticity has to do with openness—how open we are to our real talents and gifts and to bringing them out without inhibiting them," says CEO Kevin Cashman of Leadersource, a Minneapolis-based consultancy. "It also applies to an understanding of our weaknesses with ourselves and others." Such authenticity cultivates one of the most powerful lubricants for personal efficacy: trust. Organizations with high levels of trust get more things done because individuals have the power to make decisions on their own. People who are confident and supported in their work are, quite simply, more effective.

Developing this authenticity also means reckoning with what you're *not* good at. In Chapter 6, "Just Managing," we talk about creating compensatory mechanisms so that your company can grow and thrive despite your personal shortcomings. Such a mature look at bringing your shadow qualities into the light of day is vital for becoming an effective manager of others. Of course, it's never easy to face or deal with these issues—but here's a simple step toward beginning this process: ask. Ask your employees how you're doing. You're likely to discover things that will surprise you, and you're likely to learn information that will help you manage better. The simple act of asking will send an important message that you value the input of others and are acknowledging your own limitations.

There's another benefit toward becoming more authentic in your behavior. You will be reminded of how your employees' needs and goals are different from yours. Roxanne Coady ran her business on the implicit assumption that all her employees were as ambitious and vested in the success of her store as she was. "I was very demanding," she says. Because her passion kept Coady focused on a million and one pressing details, she would constantly forget to let employees know when they had done a great job. "I tend to talk only about what needs to get done," she says. When Coady had a revelation that she needed a general manager to help her manage the employees in greater detail, she learned to switch gears herself and assume a different role—that of leader more than simply manager. With that shift in emphasis, Coady recognized the importance of celebrating the small victories of her staff.

Change and Grow

Coady's growth reflects one final observation about managing others. As if it's not enough to find that hiring friends or family leads to a new set of rules that often conflict with your natural tendencies, don't ever get comfortable with how you have succeeded at this challenge. For you will find that these rules, and the mutual expectations, change as a business grows. More often than not, they change far sooner and more often than you can possibly imagine. The challenge for company-builders is to learn to hire the right people for the right stage of your venture, and to structure their working relationship to anticipate change. You must be prepared to change your people, and your mutual agreements, as the enterprise grows.

"You have a different role when you are the top person, and the collegial friendships you had when you started become more distant," says Marion McGovern, "There are new boundaries that you didn't have at the beginning." Ultimately, you will become more than the founder, the manager, or the boss: you will become *a leader*. You will have both responsibility, which is something you have to yourself, and accountability, which binds you to others. In small companies, the role of the leader is not merely to take care of details, but to create a system in which others can grow just as you have. Ultimately, as the leader of the company, you learn to enable others to achieve by establishing clear and fair policies, and by helping them align their goals with that of the company.

Here are a few final thoughts.

Leave Nothing Unsaid

The best agreements in finance and employment are simple and fair —yet they are also crystalline in terms of mutual expectations. They prepare for good times, and they anticipate that things may go bad. They spell out what each of you agree to do for one another, and they are still flexible enough to allow for growth.

Praise

This practice is simple, inexpensive, and has no negative consequences. Yet most managers forget the power of recognizing good work. Seek ways to motivate everyone in your organization by recognizing and celebrating good work at every level.

Let Go!

"When you first start out, you want people to be extensions of your own personality," says Gus Rancatore, "but then there comes a time when you allow people to do what they want to do—and you come to enjoy it."

Now that you have begun to make the most out of the others in your organization, you can take this practice to the next level by learning how to make the most of yourself as part of the company you have created. It's a small step from managing others to seeing your company as a "whole," and finding your most productive role within it.

"The best thing about working with others isn't having someone do something just the way you do. That's okay. The best thing is having someone do something *better* than you do. It would have been fine for my ice cream maker named Adam Simha to make the gianduia ice cream I developed— but it was priceless to have him make the perfect chocolate bourbon that I would never have thought of creating."

—Gus Rancatore

To paraphrase a famous quote, it's one small step for manager, one giant leap for your enterprise. Let's look at how you manage it.

RESOURCES

Leadership from the Inside Out by Kevin Cashman (Executive Excellence Publishing, Provo, Utah, 1999)

Cynics will find this book's focus on discovering your personal areas of mastery and developing the quality and authenticity to be, for lack of a better word, "touchy-feely." And that's a good thing. For managing and leading others, especially in the setting of a small business, inexorably deals with the owner's personal emotional baggage. This book helps you learn to acknowledge your own feelings and strengths—in the context of leading others.

Danger in the Comfort Zone by Judith M. Bardwick (Amacom, New York, 1991)

Bardwick's book is as "hard" as Cashman's is "soft." I've heard many entrepreneurs swear by this book, in which Bardwick argues that too many employees are driven by an ethos of entitlement— an expectation of comfort and security from their corporation irrespective of how well they perform. Such an attitude drives their bosses into a fearful defensiveness. Ultimately, both parties shy away from an environment in which individuals earn their keep, take responsibility, and face up to the consequences of their behavior. Bardwick offers helpful tactics to move both bosses and employees toward a responsible and mutually acceptable atmosphere of productive work.

The Entrepreneur's Guide to Business Law by Constance E. Bagley and Craig E. Dauchy (West Educational Publishing Company, 1998)

Bagley and Dauchy's comprehensive guide to the various legal issues you confront as a small business owner does a nice job of avoiding dry legalese. They discuss your legal considerations in the context of specific business decisions you may face, and they have a good sense of where these legal considerations fit in with the broader goal of building a business. I cite the book in this chapter because their chapter on human resources is a great, succinct guide to the various issues you need to monitor as you hire employees.

1001 Ways to Reward Your Employees by Bob Nelson (Workman Publishing, New York, 1994)

I don't care how corny this book may appear to be. Simple and direct, Nelson's book is one of the most important reminders to praise, praise, praise your employees for doing good work. Recognition may be the most important benefit of all. Nelson's plethora of tips, many of them extremely low-cost, proves that the bootstrapping ethos applies just as strongly to managing people as it does to any other resource.

6

Just Managing

I must create a system or be enslaved by another man's.
　　　—William Blake, "Jerusalem"

LEARN TO "OWN" YOUR BUSINESS—AND YOURSELF

Paul Eldrenkamp loved being a carpenter. He was so good at the trade
that word-of-mouth advertisng led to new jobs, and before he knew
it, his Boston-based company, Byggmeister, had grown into a half-
million-dollar remodeling company. Yet Eldrenkamp wasn't satisfied.
Though happy at running his own business, he was barely paying himself a salary, and the company's net profits were negligible. He also
shied away from several key tasks. Eldrenkamp didn't like selling,
and he avoided managing the business by the numbers. As a

consequence, his profitability was low, he was wasting time tracking down unprofitable leads, and he was not landing the most profitable jobs. A proficient craftsman, Eldrenkamp had let the company's product speak for itself for too long.

It took the impetus of a collective kick in the behind from members of a business network that Eldrenkamp belonged to for him to move from being owned by his business to owning it. Spurred by the other business owners, Eldrenkamp began to implement a series of changes (including how he generated new business, how he priced his jobs, and how he managed his workers) that helped him "lay down the tools" and focus on growing his company. He came to believe, as he told *Inc. Magazine*, "there's as much artistry involved in building a business as there is in building a cabinet or a house."

Such a revelation is crucial for any nascent entrepreneur. Although your business can get a huge jump out of the starting blocks by having one great product or service, you must ultimately develop overall business skills that are as proficient as your passion for your product. You must consciously move from obsessing over the smallest details of your operation to learning to become skilled at the larger questions that keep it vibrant. This means distinguishing between the strength of your product or service, and the enterprise with which you intend to capitalize on it.

Developing this well-rounded perspective requires a skill that for many entrepreneurs comes easily and for others is an acquired trait: humility, or 'fessin up to what you are not good at. As you recognize your shadow side, the question "What can't you do?" will reveal itself to be perhaps more important than an appraisal of your strengths. Sure, lightning can strike your company in all kinds of ways, but an entrepreneur who fails to address his or her limitations is courting disaster.

That's because your entrepreneurial vehicle will amplify your character flaws beyond your wildest imagination. If you are self-effacing, your company will be low profile. If you shy away from the numbers, then it's likely your company will not use its resources productively, to say the least. If you don't like confronting people, then expect your company to have sloppy dealings with its customers. It's human to have such flaws. But running a company demands that you deal with this human condition. As head of a company, you must learn to recognize these flaws and compensate for them. "Most companies tend to take on the personal characteristics of their founders. The important thing is to understand accurately your strengths and weaknesses, and fill in the weaknesses," says entrepreneur Jerry Kaplan.

Creating a balanced company also forces you to become skilled at identifying and asking for what your venture needs. Businesses need support from mentors, teachers, colleagues, customers, and even competitors. You must learn to enlist these stakeholders in your enterprise. For your company to thrive, you need support and nourishment from friends and family, peer groups, suppliers, partners, and many others. Your job now is to identify who can help you with that particular blend of advice and resources, and learn how to secure that asset.

"It is self-evident that businesses, like people, are supposed to grow; and with growth, comes change. Unfortunately, most business are not run according to this principle. Instead most businesses are operated according to what the *owner* wants as opposed to what the *business* needs."

—Michael Gerber, *The E-Myth Revisited*

"Owning" the company means learning to see your venture as a system. It means understanding how everything fits together. When hiring, for example, you don't focus solely on one person's individual talents and experience, but consider how he or she will fit with you and the other members of the team. Or you link the investment in a new computer system to the overall capacity that it gives your enterprise. Such a systematic way of thinking enables you to be more powerful as the leader of the company, without necessarily taking on more control. That's because when you can see the company as a system, then, like a garden, you can let things grow from the preparation and cultivation you have put into the enterprise.

Being responsible for everything that happens doesn't mean that you *do* everything. This is a hard lesson for many beginners, and certainly a difficult one for veteran entrepreneurs. Yet it remains critical. Any healthy business will reach a point where its demands exceed the scope of the chief, and at that point his or her efforts to control everything will hinder rather than grow the business. Your chief role then is to integrate, both internally and externally, all the resources and ideas in such a way as to create added value. And then you must delegate, compensate, and invest.

The fact that your company needs professional management doesn't necessarily mean that you have to accept this role yourself. "A lot of founders make a fatal mistake when they give up what they are good at. They may actually be a lousy manager. If someone is a master bread baker they need to have someone who is a good manager—and they stay on the bread side," says Saj-Nicole Joni, a consultant who helps businesspeople form networks of support. In other words, you gain a company by relinquishing a degree of control. Such a choice may mean that you are choosing to limit your growth, or acknowledging the natural limits to your company's size. (We'll look at this choice more in Chapter 7, "Perpetual Learning.") If you can take such a mature and self-aware attitude toward your business, you're in great shape. But you must still ensure that well-rounded practices become embedded in the organization.

This chapter will help you step back from being the center of your company's universe and help it operate efficiently and consistently on its own. You have a company with a product. You've learned how to produce it as well as how to profitably and consistently serve the needs of your customers. You've accomplished this by securing the right resources, building a productive company, and leveraging your existing resources. Now you need to implement systems and policies that enable your business to sustain itself.

Create an External Network of Support

From the very beginning, you've been forming networks to nurture your venture. The very act of being in business means cultivating

---

"The new venture has an idea. It may have a product or a service. It may even have sales, and sometimes quite a substantial volume of them. It surely has costs. And it may have revenues and even profits. What it does not have is a 'business,' a viable, operating, organized 'present' in which people know where they are going, what they are supposed to do, and what the results are or should be. But unless a new venture develops into a new business and makes sure of being 'managed,' it will not survive no matter how brilliant the entrepreneurial idea, how much money it attracts, how good its products, nor even how great the demand for them."

Peter Drucker, *Entrepreneurship and Innovation*, p. 188

customers, employees, investors, and other supporters. Yet to make the next transition, you may need to feed your business with outside input. As you turn your energies increasingly to the business of your business, your greatest tool in seeding your own growth may come from outsiders who can offer you insight and support. (See the sidebar "Where Can You Get Help?")

WHERE CAN YOU GET HELP?

Learning from experience, although critical to mastering the intimate details of your company, can only take you so far. To get better at the business of their business, many entrepreneurs find the need for outside support and counsel. For this, you can turn to a number of organized networks.

The best known and most established organizations are, *Young Entrepreneurs' Organization* (YEO) and *Young Professionals Organization* (YPO). These groups support you through regular meetings with a close group of fellow entrepreneurs who will listen to your problems, offer solutions, and, perhaps best of all, share their own stories of similar challenges. You will find solace and validation in addition to tips and advice.

YEO is a worldwide organization with 95 chapters. To join, you need to be under 40 years of age and be the owner, founder, cofounder, or controlling shareholder of a company with annual sales of $1 million or more. Membership is by invitation only. Interested candidates can submit applications through the YEO Web site (**www.yeo.org**) or you can contact YEO at 1199 N. Fairfax Street, Suite 200, Alexandria, VA 22314. Tel: (703) 519-6700, Fax: (703) 519-1864.

continues

Members of YEO must resign at the end of the fiscal year in which they turn 40. At that time, they can "graduate" to the Young Presidents Organization or the World Entrepreneurs Organization. Members must apply to the Young Presidents Organization (**www.wpo.org**) before their forty-fourth birthday. Members must hold the title of President, Chairman, Chief Executive Officer, Managing Director, Managing Partner, Publisher, or equivalent of any of the above, and must head an organization that meets certain requirements of staff size, annual revenue, and/or valuation. To apply, send inquiries to Young Presidents Organization, Att: Global Services Center, 451 S. Decker Drive, Irving, TX 75062. As for the World Entrepreneurs Organization, membership is open to executives between the ages of 39 and 44 who are the founder, cofounder, owner, or controlling shareholder of a business with annual gross sales exceeding (US)$1,000,000.

Then there's TEC (800-274-2367), an international organization that brings together entrepreneurs under the supervision of a facilitator who also meets with individuals. TEC makes a point of organizing itself across industries (CEOs are not allowed if they are direct competitors) so the focus is on managerial rather than operational issues.

Don't forget your industry trade group also. If you belong to a trade or professional association, chances are good that it has local or regional chapters. These chapters have varying degrees of affiliation with the national organization and may, as in the case of local Bar Associations, run largely independently of the national affiliate. Check your local Yellow Pages under "Professional Associations." The *Association Yellow*

continues

Book, available in your local library, is the comprehensive directory of all national trade and professional organizations.

Finally, consider such groups as your local chamber of commerce, the *National Federation of Independent Business*, and the *National Federation of Women Business Owners* (NFWBO) or the *National Association of Women Business Owners* (NAWBO.)

For Laura Peck Fennema, formal organizations of CEO support, such as the YEO, have provided invaluable assistance. "It served as an informal board of directors," she says. She discovered that many of the issues that she felt were unique challenges to her experience with Essentiel Elements were in fact common problems that other members had already encountered. By finding common ground in their struggles, she was able to resolve her problems. CEO Marion McGovern of M Squared also found in YEO a peer group of entrepreneurs who could relate to the struggles she was facing. "Other people do not go through the same stuff that the entrepreneur does," she says, adding that she found succor with "other people who were worrying about whether they could meet payroll."

McGovern realized two other benefits from participating in the small, regular meetings. First of all, her peers developed, over time, the ability to question her on important matters from her managerial choices to her commitment to maintain a work-family balance. When she was considering selling part of the company, for example, she said her circle of informal advisors pressed her on whether this move would allow her to remain true to her work-life goals. "They gave me real pause," she says. Additionally, McGovern says the structured format of the group is conducive to deeper listening and introspective participation—skills that invariably helped engender productive dialogue among her employees. "Listening without seeming judgmental in a group becomes a skill that translates to dealing with others in your company," she says.

Naturally, you can also create your network of support from available resources. Gregg Latterman of Aware Records has always relied on his business school friends from Northwestern's Kellogg School to keep him honest. "When I have questions on how to do something, no matter how technical it was, I always knew I had someone who had the answer," he says.

You can create a board of directors to keep you honest, to bring more experienced players to your company, and to form a sounding board for the company. "The board of directors is the classic check and balance," says Gary Hirshberg of Stonyfield Farm, who advises people to form a board as a safety net of people around you. Stonyfield Farm's earliest board was Hirshberg, founder Samuel Kaymen, and his wife, Louise. After a year and a half they invited their CPA to join, and in the process adapted his financial acumen (and tassled loafers) to their collective wisdom. "He got us through and then eventually we added to the board somebody who looked more acceptable to VCs," says Hirshberg.

"Somebody has to challenge the founder's appraisal of the needs of the venture, and of his own personal strengths. Someone who is not part of the problem has to ask questions, to review decisions, and, above all, to push constantly to have the long-term survival needs of the new venture satisfied by building in the market focus, supplying financial foresight, and creating a functioning top management team."

—Peter Drucker, *Innovation and Entrepreneurship*

Hirshberg also found key support from, of all people, his mother-in-law. She became a significant early investor in the company (at some points, pledging more support than her daughter realized, says Hirshberg). Yet she offered more than simple investment capital. As a real estate entrepreneur, she had developed extensive experience in understanding such key areas as the documentation process of loans. The board soon invited her to join. Although she proved a great asset in managing deals, Hirshberg always found that she provided something more important. "Her primary value was uncompromised loyalty. When things were dark she was always there."

Compensate for Your Weaknesses

The honest input of outsiders will help you come to grips with those things at which you stink. "A business really tests you and forces you to be honest," says Roxanne Coady. "If you want your business to grow, you have to ask the people you are working with what you are doing wrong. And you have to be willing to listen."

Easy, right? Never. Especially in a startup. That's because the very same traits that have enabled you to get your business up and running are often the exact same traits that keep you from seeing your flaws. Consider these traits to be your entrepreneurial shadow: the larger and brighter your personality the greater a shadow it will cast.

I like to think of acknowledging your weaknesses as *reversing the flow* of much of your early entrepreneurial activity. You stop selling and learn to listen at a deeper level than before. You consciously, deliberately take actions that may feel supremely counterintuitive to

"For the most part, entrepreneurs are characterized by public confidence and private anxiety. The public confidence helps them woo investors and customers. The private anxiety helps them build better businesses. It also helps them reach out to others because if they didn't have networks in which to share that anxiety, their heads would explode. In part, that helps explain the trendy 'entrepreneur-in-residence' at top venture capital firms. Sure, they lend expert advice to VC partners. But they're also there as a shoulder to cry on for the entrepreneurs. It's lonely to start your own business, out on a limb while doubters and naysayers buzz you and peck at your confidence. If the entrepreneur doesn't have a network, at the very least he or she should have an extremely capable psychotherapist."

—Todd Barrett, consultant to entrepreneurs

your now-comfortable role as the person who solves all problems and fixes the flaws in the system.

Starting and growing the company feel like an unending struggle. You're constantly fighting to secure resources, converting leads into customers, and staying up all night beating the product into shape. You play the hero's role in putting out fires and winning small victories. However, this hero role carries strong emotional burdens. You feel as if you need to control everything, to save others, to direct people, and solve problems as the leader. And it's hard to let go of these feelings. Even if you may be able to acknowledge the need for this shift, emotionally you will find it nearly impossible to give up control. But you must.

One of the important ways that you must face your organizational weaknesses is the feedback of others. Ask your partners, colleagues, or investors what you are doing well and, more importantly,

where you are failing the company. Large corporations have something called 360-degree feedback, in which employees have the
opportunity to evaluate the performance of their boss. This is but one
useful tool in assessing your weaknesses.

Be sure to seek the input of a disinterested party. In the early
days of Stonyfield Farm, Gary Hirshberg judged his skills as compared to founder Samuel Kaymen. "I prided myself on being Samuel's
counterpoint," says Hirshberg. "He was completely idealistic and
reckless in his treatment of people and his spending habits." Yet the
"Samuel standard" kept Hirshberg from realizing that simply having
more financial controls than his partner didn't qualify him as a well-
rounded chief. "I'd developed a self-image as someone who was the
manager. But in so doing I allowed myself to become a self-
caricature. I forget that I too was very idealistic and that my idealism
often got us in a bad jam," Hirshberg says. It took the counsel of outsiders, some of whom eventually joined the company's board, to help
him see where his true strengths and weaknesses were.

Learning to come to terms with your shadow side helps you take
the next logical step: compensating. "Delegating becomes really
easy once you figure out what you are good at and what you are not
good at," according to Hirshberg.

Hirshberg was fortunate to realize early on that he couldn't do
a number of important duties at the company as well as others. "I
was not good at the detailed follow-through of tracking results, keeping records, or making sure that I had analyzed the very best insurance policies and the like," he says. Hirshberg turned to his controller
for help. "My first controller wore many hats," he says. "He was the
chief of human resources, for example, and kept track of a number
of administrative functions." Delegating these areas enabled

Hirshberg to focus on those things that he knew he was good at, such as raising capital, selling, marketing, and managing people. Not coincidentally, Stonyfield Farm can trace much of its growth and success to its strengths in these very areas. The company's strong values have served as an effective marketing tool that has given it a high profile, and it has leveraged its success by slowly expanding its product lines.

What can you afford to delegate and what do you need to keep your hands on? There's no magic formula. You should mete out duties only after a careful assessment of your strengths and weaknesses. Always ask how this will affect the organization as a whole rather than you as an individual.

Delegating is easier said than done. There's no point in delegating responsibility to others without ceding enough control to them to do the job on their own. The important consideration when entrusting others with work you once handled yourself is to give them enough space to get the work done, yet construct a mechanism by which you can monitor their success, and offer coaching when they need help. Larger companies often use financial targets as a common language of business success; you too should find measures that track success that enable you and your colleagues to assess their performance in a systematic manner.

For delegating to be successful, you need to learn to trust others. This sounds simple—but it's one of the toughest mental attitudes for a company founder to cultivate. That's because trusting others to get things done the right way naturally conflicts with so many of the beliefs and attitudes that helped you launch the company.

Founder and owner Cynthia Rivera Hunt, who started Applause Designs in 1998, a Web-based retailer of personalized candy wrappers for corporations and special events, found that letting even part-time employees become very familiar with the workings of her business proved much harder than she expected. "You don't want them to divulge any trade secrets," she says. "Call it paranoia, but you have worked very hard and put your heart and soul into this business. You're very protective of what you have created."

This impulse arose naturally from her protectiveness about the company. "I wanted to make sure the people who help me care about the business as much as I do in making a good product," says Hunt. Initially, she was nervous about sharing her work with outsiders. Yet over time, she gradually learned to build trust. "I realized they were interested in what I was doing and thought it was a really cool business." Moreover, she learned that developing trust is a process that builds on itself. You learn to trust others by simply trusting them. "It all comes down to practice," she says, "I just need to get my feet wet."

The issue of trust runs deeper than simply trusting other individuals. Eventually, you must learn to trust the organization. Once you have given others the authority to make decisions, to develop new products, and to have latitude with customers, then get out of the way. Creating a system where others have responsibilities without authority is a recipe for failure.

Accept Your New Role

Finally, implementing systems and polices and delegating matters to people who can handle them more effectively or more cost-effectively than you enables you (forces you, but let's not quibble) to take a new role. Although you need to remain aware of the daily operations, you now have the power and responsibility to keep focused on the most important matters facing your company.

Such a role may feel ill-fitting at first. Gus Rancatore found the transition bittersweet. "One of the pleasures of growing your business is doing different things," he says. "Today I miss making as much ice cream as I used to." Although he doesn't mind mopping the floors, he still longs for the simpler pleasures of spending hours refining a new batch of sorbet.

"You see what you are not good at and then try to improve that or recognize limitations, and then outsource things if need be. For me, it has forced me to be more organized and to look for solutions outside myself. In a big company, I could, say, bring in a good manager. In a little company, it means making good use of an accountant and computers." He has created a simple structure for the store. Employees who used to be generalists break down into scoopers or ice cream makers, and rarely do the two converge. He counts on employees to handle bookkeeping functions that he once thought he needed to control.

"Shifting hours has allowed me to concentrate more on training and marketing and the day part of the business," he says. At the same time, the new role never feels completely "right" inside. It's his business, and he can handle most aspects better than most of his employees. But what the store needs now is for him to convert these skills into teaching assets. "I want to do that, and yet I bemoan the loss of ice cream-making time." Rancatore will never completely give up being a flavor alchemist, yet he is learning to find another form of satisfaction in helping train others to come up with the next great flavor. (See the sidebar "Where Do You Need Help?")

Manage by Choice!

The net result of implementing systems and polices that free you from the onerous job of running the show single-handedly is *managing by*

WHERE DO YOU NEED HELP?

As you grow as a manager, you should find yourself moving from managing by tasks (which is the definition of *micromanaging* and can make you and your employees miserable if taken to extremes) to managing by objectives. This involves you and your employees working together toward goals you all understand and share.

Try this exercise. Take a sheet of paper and draw a vertical line down the middle, making two columns. In the right-hand column, describe your own perfect working day, starting from the time you get to work to the time you leave for the day. List the things you would do and—just as important—the things you wouldn't need to do if you ran the universe.

Fold the sheet of paper in half, so that the right column is hidden. In the left-hand column, list all the things that *need* to be done over the course of the day to make your business run—everything from listening to voicemail messages to taking out the trash.

Then—you guessed it—compare the left column to the right. Anything that shows up on the left side of the paper, but isn't a part of your ideal day, is an area where you should consider asking for help.

Repeat this process for your perfect month, your perfect quarter, and your perfect year, replacing shorter-term tasks (such as ordering supplies or filing tax returns) with longer-term projects or objectives (such as publishing a catalog or turning over inventory).

The brutal truth is that most of us spend time on the things we enjoy and feel we're good at, and avoid the things we don't enjoy or feel we aren't good at. You'll never be able to free yourself from every unpleasant duty, but one of the major benefits of being the boss is being able to hire people to do the things that you don't want to do. Believe it or not, there's someone out there who *enjoys* doing the things you hate to do—or who at least may be willing to do the things you hate to do for the chance to do something better.

choice. You run the company by choice, by design, rather than by putting out fires.

Roxanne Coady had to make many mistakes before implementing a mission statement and more formal policies and procedures. Although she always knew why she wanted to start a bookstore, Coady could only think through the values and mission of her company long after it was up and running. "I think when you start a business you are almost in a fog—and I think that when I emerged from that fog I started assessing things differently. Only after we reached a certain level could I begin institutionalizing policies and procedures that before you addressed on an ad hoc basis."

Sometime after her insight that she had let her passion for the book business cloud her judgment as a businessperson, Coady began a more formal process of examining and articulating what the company stood for. With her employees, the company redrafted the mission and values statement—and, more importantly, began using this constitution as a basis for decisions.

The process of institutionalizing policies and procedures that had previously been ad hoc practices was a delicate one. "How do you stop from being a loveless giant?" Coady wondered. Intriguingly, Coady found that these core principles helped enlist her employees

"There's an irony to having your own business. On the one hand, you have more freedom than ever, but on the other, you are more burdened than you could ever imagine. CEOs don't have power; they are always running to appease the stakeholders. And in small companies you are likewise forever burdened with your million and one responsibilities."

—Roxanne Coady, R. J. Julia Books

in the broader goal of the company and helped Coady take on a more active role with matters outside the company. Recently, for example, she took her involvement in the American Booksellers Association to a new level, by accepting the key role of treasurer. Such a move was made possible by her confidence in the store's ability to grow without her micromanagement.

The challenge is to build systems and controls that further the values and systems rather than stifle it. You want to retain the spirit of a small business while tapping the benefits of professional management. Creating an infrastructure can cripple a company when it squeezes the life out of it. The challenge is to merge the new controls with the core values and mission of the company. This enables you to pass on your heart and spirit from an individual level to that of the enterprise.

In so doing, you move from the role of heroic entrepreneur to a key player in a team that is aligned by the goals of the company. Author and coach Kevin Cashman says that many companies fall down when it comes time for this transition. Most entrepreneurial organizations have a heroic leadership model, he says. "By virtue of the founder's vision, they are going to get something important done." Yet he says that the primary motivating force in this system emanates from the entrepreneur rather than the company. "People get connected to an entrepreneur not because they are developing great systems, but as a result of their charisma and sense of purpose and meaning. It is often more about their vision than about the system," he says. This can only work for so long. "Unfortunately, people can be retained by that approach for a certain amount of time only. But then they seek a sense of connection with their teammates—and the systems to support this sense of teamwork."

Here are some final thoughts.

Be Brutally Honest with Yourself

Placing your stake and that of others into a business raises the stakes of your behavior exponentially. The consequences of your inability to deal with operational details, to learn the finer points of debt service, or to confront the failings of an employee or partner will be far greater than if you were simply running solo. Building a vehicle around your passion puts more at stake, and you are compelled to face —and address—your weaknesses.

Get Comfortable Asking for Help

Your business needs everything from financing to advice to moral support, a condition that will only increase over time. Some entrepreneurs are born salespeople, or feel no compunction about asking others for anything. But all company founders and builders must become proficient at identifying and then securing what they need from others.

Now you've begun to develop the systems and mechanisms so that your company can sustain itself. You've tapped into outside networks, created internal resources, and developed a new mindset that trains your thinking on what your company needs. Now let's look at how you go to the next step.

RESOURCES

The E-Myth Revisited by Michael Gerber (HarperBusiness, New York, 1995)

"The technical work of a business and a business that does technical work are two totally different things!" says Gerber, who argues that the vast majority of entrepreneurs who launch companies based

on a technical expertise eventually find themselves hating that expertise. "Knowing the technical work of their business becomes their single greatest liability." According to Gerber, technologists who found companies take on a dozen jobs that they hate, chores that distract them from their calling. Unless they can find a way to integrate the function of manager with that of entrepreneur and technologist, their company will fail. This didactic book has found a huge and devoted audience through its sensible insight into how all entrepreneurs must evolve—or step aside.

"Taming the Beast" by David Whitford (*Inc. Magazine,* April 1996. Access it through **www.inc.com**.)

It's rare to find a magazine article with the depth and wisdom of a full-length book. Yet this piece by veteran journalist David Whitford gives a rich account of how entrepreneur Paul Eldrenkamp made the painful transition from being owned by his business to owning it. Not just a source of information, this article can help inspire you to confront the emotional and practical barriers to growth that are created by your love for your business.

Trust in the Balance by Robert Bruce Shaw (Jossey-Bass, San Francisco, 1997)

Managers develop trust in organizations through achieving business results, acting with integrity, and demonstrating concern, says Shaw. He shows how trust grows dynamically when leaders place trust in individuals—who are given the means to earn that trust through performing. Shaw skews toward larger companies, yet his advice on cultivating a high-trust culture is very germane—perhaps more so—to small companies.

7

Perpetual Learning

Ah, but I was so much older then,
I'm younger than that now.
—Bob Dylan, "My Back Pages"

LEARN TO BE A LIFELONG LEARNER

Marion McGovern thinks a lot these days about what she calls "parenting the company." Today M Squared has grown into a healthy, thriving enterprise that has realized her vision of a successful interim talent agency. During these past 12 years, McGovern has found that her role has gradually evolved, and that her role as a mother of three children is the best analogy for the way her relationship with the company has grown.

"There's an intimacy you have with the startup that is very different than the intimacy you have with the adolescent," says McGovern. "In the early days, you know how it breathes and burps," she says, explaining that one's identity becomes inexorably mixed in with this new entity. As the creator and protector of a new baby, you have to take care of every last consideration for this helpless thing. You more or less identify completely.

And then, says McGovern, at some level you start recognizing that you are separate entities. With her business, for example, she took pride as it began to acquire the ability to talk back to her, to make its own decisions, to take matters into its own hands. Like a child, the business took on a life of its own that she couldn't quite control. "In the early days, the company is really an extension of your personality, but when it grows, it takes on its own personality, kind of like when an infant asserts its own independence," she says. At that point the difficult challenge is to learn when to let go—how to step back increasingly and focus on broader strategic areas while others dealt with immediate company concerns.

This journey has been filled with many meaningful blunders on her part. She observes that this path includes the painful mistakes one learns as a parent. "The kids fall down and get hurt and they keep going. You make mistakes and you learn from them," she says. "Kids are always skinning their knees. The hope is that you figure out the time the child is really sick and needs the doctor and this is the flu." Her simple hope is that she has built in the appropriate systems and policies for the company to learn on its own. "If you take the kid analogy, as they get closer to thriving on their own, they have got to be able to interpret events and situations in the way you think you've prepared them." Today McGovern still cares deeply about her company. She just tends it very differently.

McGovern has learned that the process of growing a company grows you as a person—that it teaches you business skills *and* skills for coping with life. Yet success can never be defined as a static place, a finish line, an end to the challenges. As one's company matures into a more viable and established presence, then your role as founder or chief continues to evolve as well. You are presented with a fresh set of challenges and opportunities. The trick is to continue to grow.

Many accomplished company builders realize that entrepreneurship is not merely about starting a business, but represents an orientation toward your entire life. "Building a business is just one vehicle for an entrepreneurial life," says Jim Collins. You start with a blank canvas and, through your own resourcefulness and ingenuity, create something new.

This challenge never stops. For many entrepreneurs, success brings you back to where you started. You once again have a dream and an outlook, and look for a vehicle through which to realize your passions. It might be your existing business. Or it might lie elsewhere. The challenge is to see through the success of your company and take it to the next level. Prosperity can too easily lead to complacency, and good entrepreneurs always keep their eye—and mind—open to new possibilities.

This challenge is rarely about wealth. Successful entrepreneurs are not motivated simply to get rich. They create wealth as a by-product of successfully realizing their dream. Focusing only on wealth as a measure of success dooms you on two counts. A strict focus on numbers alone distracts you from some of the more meaningful reasons you started the company in the first place. You will also be more likely to never be satisfied with even great riches.

This chapter will help you think through how to take your accumulated wisdom and experience to the next level, as well as how to think about whether you want to continue to grow the company—or not. Or whether it's time to start another. Or whether it's simply time to fold up and move to the next thing. Or whether you want to cash out. Many different ways are available for using your new station as a means of growing your company and yourself. This may mean reinventing your business. It may mean stepping aside to take a different role as the company grows beyond your capacity. And it may mean moving on.

Regardless, your passions and dreams will still guide your path. To grow continually, you must be willing to give up your familiar notions and models of success and find new ways to realize your passion through your enterprise. Here's how.

REVISIT YOUR MISSION

Once your business is profitable, has a healthy cash flow, has established a solid customer base, and displays a capacity to run on its own, you need to take a step back to revisit the original mission of your company. Ask yourself whether you are continuing to realize that goal. How well has your company realized its potential? Your company has probably evolved considerably from your original conception of a business. Now you need to take a step back and ask yourself dispassionately: how do I continue to realize the original vision?

To do so will almost certainly require resources from outside your current position. This requires outside help. Just as you developed a network to help you form the company and to develop the resources (such as finance and assets and contacts) to grow, now you need to form a network to help you continue to grow at your new level. Your needs and capabilities have changed since you launched your company, and so may your sources of support. In Chapter 6, "Just Managing," we talked about how many entrepreneurs find comfort and nourishment in such organizations as YEO or TEC. These networks can also help you address the broader challenges of growth.

The simplest way of growing your company while sticking to your vision is simply extending what you do. Leading business thinkers like to talk about "core competence," which basically means the stuff you are really good at. Stonyfield Farm, for example, is really good at making great-tasting products from natural and organic farm foods, and producing them in an environmentally conscious manner. Although the company has ventured into nonyogurt products, such as sour cream and eggnog, over the years it has tapped into its basic strengths to grow yogurt into an ever-growing family of products. Today the company offers children's and baby yogurt, frozen yogurt, soy-based yogurt, and, yes, one crazy nonyogurt product—ice cream.

SEEK THE RIGHT MEASURE OF GROWTH

Growth, pure growth, is not necessarily a good thing. To remain aligned with your vision and mission, you may very well have to make tradeoffs in terms of size. You've learned that revenue growth without cash flow can kill your business. And there's a broader corollary: Excessive company growth can turn your business into a very different entity than you envisioned, or want. That's why growth can and must be managed if you want the company to stay healthy and focused on the right things.

Amy Miller of Amy's Ice Cream has always made a conscious decision to keep her company at a manageable level. "Growth is wise only when accomplished with an understanding of what makes your business concept competitive and sustainable," she says. In the early days of her business, Miller was constantly pushed by outsiders to grow the company as fast as possible. She had developed a huge and loyal audience, and potential investors and fans often wanted more.

Yet Miller borrowed a lesson on growth from a parallel life of hers at the time—that of a competitive boxer. Miller had always been athletic and took up boxing as therapy after suffering a running injury. After training in the sport for several years, she fought her first match and received considerable media attention and support. Miller then turned down inquiries to quickly push a professional career. "The risks of professional boxing were so physical and so immediate that I was able to listen to my gut rather than to my supporters' cries for more," she says in an essay titled "The Knockout Lesson." "I wasn't avoiding a challenge. I was taking measured risks I felt would lead me best toward *my* idea of success."

Miller chose to open stores carefully, to give each new location a distinctive identity rather than duplicate a prototype. This enabled her to respond with more precision to different markets, and to continue to learn about how to bring in new design choices. She has never regretted this strategy. "Slow growth with an emphasis on our system design is the strategy that's most consistent with my skills, my motives for being in business, my instinct for what makes the company successful, and my risk comfort level. My experiences with boxing allowed me to see clearly that it is only you who will be hurt if, contrary to your own best judgement, you follow the crowd."

Laura Peck Fennema has also kept her foot off the gas pedal with Essentiel Elements. For the first 10 years or so of her company, Fennema avoided a growth rate of more than 20 to 25 percent a year. "I didn't want to grow it so fast because then we would have had to go out and find capital," she says, "and the whole reason I was doing this was to have fun." Fennema believed that she would have had to sacrifice too much control by giving up equity. "I was doing this as something I had a distinct passion for, and I didn't want to be pressured by the rate of return criteria of the venture community," she says. By growing at a pace in the 10 to 15 percent range, that the company could fund internally, Fennema continues to own more than a majority of the company, and she has gotten a deeper emotional reward as well. "Frankly, it was a more rewarding experience for me —it enabled me to grow at a pace that was manageable and fun."

Of course, you may not have such a conscious decision about limiting growth. Many businesses often reach a plateau beyond which they cannot grow. You may be limited by your geographic location, your market niche, or your available resources. Going to the next step may require the same time and emotional commitment that it took to get you started in the first place. In fact, there may be possibly more risk, because now you have something to lose! So be prepared. If you decide to grow beyond your current scope, you may well be inviting new challenges and risks that you couldn't have imagined as a startup.

REVISIT YOUR ROLE

One of the biggest threats is that your company will outgrow you. Growth will force you to ask yourself whether you're still the right person to lead the company. Ask yourself what the company—rather than you—needs. Because it's very likely that the time will come when you will need to seriously reconsider your role—if any—with the company you've created from nothing.

As your company grows, your role in it naturally evolves as well. In Chapter 6, we looked at mechanisms that help you find the optimal position in the company, one that leverages your natural strengths by matching them to your business's needs. But should your company grow beyond your original scope, you may need to consider taking an entirely different role. Companies often require different leaders as they grow and change.

"Entrepreneurs have to perform different tasks and play different roles to build long-lived firms than they do when they start businesses. Their predisposition and their capacity to perform these tasks depend on a different set of qualities. The willingness of entrepreneurs to adopt audacious goals for their firms depends on the nature of their ambition and their tolerance for risk . . . .

"The limited correlation between the qualities involved in starting and building businesses helps explain why so few new ventures become long-lived institutions. Success at the startup stage depends on an individual's capacity for opportunistic adaptation. Traits and skills such as a tolerance for ambiguity, perceptiveness, tactical ingenuity, and capacity for face-to-face selling help determine which new ventures build a large, durable business and the tolerance for the requisite sacrifices and risks. Then, from the ranks of the ambitious, the forces of competition leave standing those very select firms whose principals have (or can develop) the capacity to formulate and implement a sound, long-term strategy. The evolution of the long-lived firm turns on the effort of truly exceptional entrepreneurs."

—Amar Bhide, *The Origin and Evolution of New Businesses*, p. 315

In his classic book *Managing Corporate Lifecycles*, consultant Ichak Adizes argues that companies grow in a similar manner. They begin with the early "courtship" phase in which the owner falls in love with the idea of the company, and then they pass through the Infancy and Go-Go phases, the frenzied startup time in which the company gets up and running. Finally, healthy companies reach the saner stage of corporate Adolescence, all of which is a prelude to what Adizes calls Prime, a healthy and mature stage of balanced creativity and discipline. Companies in prime are mature, effective, and profitable businesses capable of sustainable growth and renewal. Unfortunately, few founders remain with their companies throughout their entire life cycle.

Now, although I'm not advocating that you start charting where your company may lay along this helpful time line, the salient point to understand here is how your company's growth may very well exceed your capacity to run the show effectively. Adizes has a name for this situation: the Founder's Trap. "From courtship through the Go-Go stages of the lifecycle, founders are their companies, and the companies are their founders. They are inseparable. When young companies need bank loans, their founders must pledge personal assets. Banks perceive founder and company as a single entity," Adizes says. Yet this condition can lead to conflict: "Companies outgrow the founder's capabilities to implant their personal leadership styles and philosophies. They can no longer act as one-person shows. That's when founders attempting to delegate authority and responsibility end up decentralizing and losing control. It usually does not work well."

Adizes argues that the strengths of the founders in getting the company up and running are invariably blatant weaknesses in running

a more mature enterprise. The same will and determination that get things done in the early days can undermine the systematic organization of others. When faced with the need to delegate decisions and responsibilities, founders often resist letting go of control and end up with a self-destructive organization—a company in which managers are given ostensible responsibility for getting things done, but little real power to take charge.

The challenge at this point, Adizes argues, is for the founder to recognize his or her limits and find a new role. Perhaps you can learn to delegate authority, develop broad rules and policies, and shift into a different emotional approach toward your company. Most founders can't. At this point, your challenge is to either move on or take a different position in the company. There's nothing wrong with becoming chief technical officer (if you founded the company on a great product) or head of sales, yet few founders have an easy time wrestling with what feels like a huge concession.

Those that do, however, have many options open to them.

The first is simply to sell and move on. Naturally, this choice never comes easily, nor does the act of leaving a company that you've founded feel very good. When Ann Handley and her partner Andy Bourland completed the transaction of selling ClickZ and finally left the company, Handley was taken aback by the emotional impact of the move. "I was surprised by the emotional part of selling the company," says Handley. "It was really very hard. Building the company was such an important experience, and it had become such a big part of me. And when the new owners said bye, it felt like breaking with an old boyfriend, one who was not necessarily good for you but who you miss at some level nonetheless."

Finally, of course, there's the sad but sometimes necessary choice of closing a company that just isn't working. This never comes easily, but, for the sake of creating a truly great company, you may have to learn from the lessons of a good but not successful one. (See the sidebar "Learning from Failure".)

JUST LIKE STARTING OVER

Even when you have taken your company as far as you want it to go, and want to retain some control over the business, some entrepreneurs simply cannot resist starting another venture. Specialists have come up with a fancy phrase to describe those feisty individuals who found more than one company: lunatics. Oops—I meant to say *serial entrepreneurs*. People who love the startup phase of companies thrill

---

LEARNING FROM FAILURE

Every month *Inc. Magazine* publishes an obituary of a business. These financial autopsies of companies gone bust don't revel in failure. The owners mentioned aren't stupid, greedy, or inept. They are often smart operators who simply ran into one of the many lurking dangers that can suddenly sink an otherwise successful company. Markets shift faster than a company can adapt. Capital dries up. A key client folds. Technology topples the industry business model. These obits show that even the best businesspeople face change and uncertainty beyond their control, and that even well-run businesses have a natural life span. So, the only way to enable your company to thrive as a living thing is to nurture your open mind.

in creating something from nothing, staying on long enough to ensure that the new venture will succeed, and then move on to the next challenge.

In 2000, after spending 12 years growing Nantucket Nectars into a nationally known company, Tom First and Tom Scott gave up day-to-day operations of their juice company in order to launch a new venture. Shelflink, their new company, was a horse of an entirely different color. In many ways, the startup was about as fundamentally different from their juice company as possible. Nantucket Nectars was bootstrapped for years; Shelflink was fueled with more than $8 million in venture capital funding. Nantucket Nectars was a bright, tasty consumer product that benefited from the young men's colorful personalities and marketing savvy. Shelflink is a technical service that helps other businesses manage their distribution needs.

Specifically, Shelflink consists of an electronic ordering service for the myriad small retailers that sell their products. Vendors who hook up with Shelflink are provided with PCs that are connected to the Web and that have a Shelflink site. They then use the Shelflink system to track orders, monitor inventory, and restock from distributors.

In Shelflink, the Toms aren't trying to effect radical change on the distribution system. They just want to give the players in the system a new set of tools to make them far more efficient. It's a smart, calculated extension of their working knowledge to a new company. First explains that their foray into this new venture made perfect sense as a natural extension of their entrepreneurial spirit. Their experience in building Nantucket Nectars provided the perfect platform for Shelflink. Their new venture arose directly out of a need they saw in the industry they worked in—specifically, an inefficient distribution system for the many small stores that purchased their products. With Shelflink, they saw an opportunity to remedy a problem they discovered through their thorough knowledge of an industry. "When we started the company, we would keep track of our accounts by using a marine radio," says First. "And now we are trying to recreate when we were intimately related in such an immediate way."

Tom Scott holds no illusions about the different type of entrepreneurial voyage that the second trip promises. "It can't be as fun," he says of the second venture. "We had fun going down the river with Nantucket Nectars, but we didn't know what was around the bend." Scott, who believes that "innocence plays an important role in entrepreneurship," doesn't want to recreate the challenges of the initial company. To do so would be like re-experiencing some of the painful moments of one's childhood. "A lot of building a company is personal stuff," he says. "You learn to be yourself."

Although you can't learn to be yourself twice, you can start anew. And so the two are continuing to pursue what Tom First calls the distracted impatience of an entrepreneur. "Once you achieve something, you are always looking at the next level," he says. Launching Shelflink was a concession on the part of the partners that their next challenge lay beyond taking Nantucket Nectars further. "It's all about the trip," Scott says. "We seek the intellectual challenge of being put in a situation where you have to figure something out, have to make something from nothing. I like it when my heart is pounding when I go to sleep at night."

Stonyfield Farm CEO Gary Hirshberg has also found new outlets for his passion to create new ventures and to realize his dream of a socially responsible business. Four years ago Hirshberg founded the Social Venture Institute (SVI), a nonprofit group that holds an annual conference to help mentor young entrepreneurs in the issues of growing a business with certain values. Hirshberg calls SVI a "boot camp" for early entrepreneurs. "We help people face the fact that most business problems are personal problems and that you aren't inventing anything new when you have these problems," he says.

Such an endeavor has helped Hirshberg mentor and nurture socially responsible companies, and has given him a chance to learn more about the challenges facing other companies with goals similar to his. In this aspect he is both teaching—and learning—at the same time.

Hirshberg also continues to feed his restless energy for completely new companies. In the spring of 2001, Hirshberg and two cofounders launched O Naturals, an all-natural alternative to such fast-food chains as McDonald's and Burger King. Hirshberg's modest goal is to create a chain of fast food outlets that serves natural and organic foods, supports communities by hosting local gatherings, and supports the practice of recycling and sustainable living. The first store opened in Falmouth, Maine, in May 2001.

GET INVOLVED IN LARGER ISSUES

Of course, you can also learn and grow without turning your company into GE. You can simply achieve greater goals while keeping your role as leader of the company. These goals, however, may simply leverage the clout you have developed through the vehicle of your company.

Many successful entrepreneurs choose to become involved in external issues tied to their company's mission. That's how Laura Peck Fennema has found ways to further her passion for botanical body care products. Fennema formed Essentiel Elements as a result of this passion. She had always cared about the therapeutic power of

ENLIST OTHERS ON YOUR VOYAGE

What's the best way to continue your personal growth while growing a business? Jim Collins has created a wonderfully useful device that helps him in his quest for continued self-actualization: a personal board of directors. Comprised of seven individuals that Collins deeply respects, this board provides advice and support on his most important life decisions. Collins turns to his board for handling crises, ethical dilemnas, and the simple big decisions that cross his path.

He recommends to others that they form a seven-person board from a diverse range of backgrounds—in particular enlisting people from outside your particular industry—in order to provide insight beyond the boundaries of your field. These individuals can bring deep perspective and wisdom to you at a time when you have lost your own perspective as a function of being completely wrapped up in running your business. Their advice can help you reconcile your current position with your broader aspirations.

"What kind of a person do you want to be? The very process of assembling and making good use of a personal board is a conscious, deliberate step toward answering that question and, most important, living by it," says Collins.

natural remedies, and, today, as a result of her company's success, Fennema has a powerful platform to take her passion a step further.

Recently, her company began to support the cultivation of distillation gardens in Sonoma, California. "This goes to one of the core ideologies of the company, which holds that our products will be the

purest on the marketplace," she says. "Since one of our core tenets is purity, it helps me to broaden the definition of what my role is." The distillation garden is a square acre of land in Sonoma that is dedicated to growing private reserves of herbs like lavender and rosemary, which can be distilled at the farm to produce the freshest and highest-quality oils.

"These kinds of projects are the type of things I would have loved to do 10 years ago had the business not consumed me so much," she says today. "In the beginning it was how do we keep the lights on. Now the question is how do we position the company as a leader in the industry?"

A few last thoughts:

WRITE YOUR PERSONAL AND YOUR BUSINESS OBITUARY

Try this slightly corny, though useful exercise. Keep in mind that obituaries don't focus on the cause of death. They discuss what the person accomplished. Obituaries share the significance of a person's life, revealing the actions, and relevance of what they accomplished. So, ask yourself: have you—and has your business—realized what you meant to do? And, if not, how will you change today to make that happen?

STAY CONNECTED TO PEOPLE OUTSIDE THE COMPANY

Although a strong company culture is usually a good sign, it runs the danger of vaccinating itself against hard truths. That's why you need to seek the counsel of outsiders whom you respect in both bad times and good in order to continue to grow.

GET A LIFE!

"Growing a business grows you as a person—it teaches you how to be a better business person," says Saj-Nicole Joni, "but it doesn't help you with personal growth." Managing people has probably taught you how critical it is to avoid intimacy in the work place, to set certain boundaries, and respect them religiously. Such compartmentalization applies to your personal life as well. You need to get away from the business, to develop an identity and self that isn't completely wrapped up in your company.

"Most people in startups work too much and they work too hard," says Gus Rancatore, who to this day vividly remembers the first time he took a day off from Toscanini's. "It was September, and my friends scooped me up and drove west on the Mass. Turnpike to look at leaves and relax. I remember hyperventilating in the back seat, thinking, 'My goodness, what if the second person doesn't come in or he forgets to call in the Monday dairy order or they don't rotate the ice cream . . .'" What if? he kept asking himself. "I was sitting in

---

"Working too much has its good points. You save money because you never spend any because you're always at work. This, the savvy small businessperson thinks, reduces labor costs. And you do develop a complete sense of the business's daily rhythms. But it's a pace that can't be kept up indefinitely. People need time away from work, and even time away from each other. They need to rewind and balance the emotional demands of work with something else. They also need something else altogether. They need to see what's happening in the outside world and continue to evolve their take on the culture and where it might be heading."

—Gus Rancatore

a car full of friends, on my first full day away from the newly hatched store and I knew I had a problem."

It took years for Rancatore to come to terms with the success of his store—to learn to place his identity as the owner of a popular ice cream store within a sense of self that included his other facets. "Running a business is in part a creative and a synthesizing activity and if you spend all your hours within the same four walls making sure that no one ever throws out four ounces of chocolate or four ounces of cream, you will get stale," says Rancatore. "Hard work, even crazy work is okay . . . up to a point. And that point is where you burn yourself out, where you diminish your effectiveness as a manager and where you lose the joy that has to be at least intermittently present. Not every moment or every day is an unalloyed joy, but you will significantly diminish the business by mutilating yourself."

Today Rancatore makes a conscious effort to keep up his interests outside the store. He takes Chinese lessons, sits on the board of a local movie theater company, and is involved in many civic events. Naturally, functions like serving ice cream at city events or helping with the planning process of his part of the city have a direct (or indirect) benefit to his store. Yet Rancatore now also pursues his outside life for his own benefit.

"Too many entrepreneurs are so focused on the business to the point that they have no life, which is tragic," says Marion McGovern. "As a married Mom in the YEO set, I can't tell you how weird (or unique if we want to be PC) I appeared to the others. As a consequence, I got asked some of the most personal and sad questions about relationships and families. Once when I asked a peer when he would consider marrying his long-term girlfriend he said, 'At around ten.' After further discovery, I learned the '10' referred to $10 million in sales.

Throughout building a company and a family, McGovern has tried to live by a simple precept: "Work is a passion and it is intrinsic to satisfaction, but it should enable our life—and not the other way around."

RESOURCES

Startup by Jerry Kaplan (Houghton Mifflin, New York, 1994)

This book is my favorite narrative account of someone launching a business. Written by a technical wizard who became possessed with the idea of creating a company—and industry—based on handheld computing, Kaplan's tale is instructive on many levels. Not merely for the nuts-and-bolts material it delivers on how money gets raised and spent in high-tech circles, but also for the personal and emotional insights that accompany "The Ride."

So why doesn't it belong, say, in the Resources in Chapter 1, "Finding Your Calling"? Because Kaplan charts the emotional journey he traveled as his prospective company raised $75 million, took baby steps toward viability . . . and failed. Wisely, Kaplan scaled a steep learning curve in the process and shares the myriad lessons he picked up on the way. A great story of learning from failure (though some would just call his adventure a practice run for a successful company).

Managing Corporate Lifecycles by Ichak Adizes (Prentice Hall Press, Paramus, New Jersey, 1999)

Adizes's target audience of consultants and organizational change leaders may not match with your early company concerns, yet his fundamental point represents a cautionary note for the future.

Adizes points out that companies go through a natural growth cycle, which often runs at a different pace from the learning capacity of the company founder. By alerting yourself to this phenomenon, learning to spot the early warning signs, and anticipating your options when faced with this juncture, you can certainly mitigate some of the pain.

The Origin and Evolution of New Businesses by Amar Bhide (Oxford University Press, New York, 2000)

A very academic book that is nonetheless one of the most insightful about how companies are formed and grow. Drawing from a wealth of case histories that he has prepared as a professor at Harvard Business School and Columbia University, Bhide reveals the varied paths your specific business can take.

The Fifth Discipline: The Art and Practice of the Learning Organization by Peter Senge (Doubleday/Currency, New York, 1990)

Some business thinkers joke that Senge's book is the best-selling classic that nobody has read. *The Fifth Discipline* has earned a reputation as a difficult read because it takes such an ambitious crack at defining the disciplines necessary for individuals and groups to learn collectively. It can be a tough book, but I heartily endorse that you read it nonetheless. At the heart of this book, Senge helps you learn to manage as a creative act rather than a reactive one. In the context of your business, he helps you move from simply putting out fires to aspiring to and realizing higher goals. Managers (and entrepreneurs) can learn and grow through the process of growing a company. They can do so joyfully and creatively for the good, argues Senge. It's a message I endorse wholeheartedly.

This book has one more great gift to entrepreneurs. At the heart of practicing organizational learning is the art of systems thinking, which is the art of seeing how different agents are ultimately related to one another—how cause and effect are related in the larger picture. Such a holistic view of a system is naturally afforded to the entrepreneur, whose system is often smaller and more immediate. Although managers in large companies may have a more complicated set of people and conditions to integrate, they nonetheless play a similar role as an entrepreneur: seeing the big picture and helping all the players create more by understanding how they all fit together.

APPENDIX

FINAL THOUGHTS

If there's one point above all that I want to make in this book, it's this: *you* can start a company. Right now, at this very minute as you read this book, you have what it takes to start your own business. You don't need a professional background, wads of cash, or the technical chops to produce a semiconductor in your garage. You don't need an MBA or a Ph.D. or the home phone number of a venture capitalist. You don't need big company background.

Sure, any or all of those credentials can help, but they aren't essential for you to start your company.

Here's what you do need: passion, commitment, and you need to care. You need to care, deeply, about your company. If you do, then you can succeed. Skills: you can acquire those. Experience: that will come. Contacts, capital, expertise: all these you can learn or acquire. If I've learned anything from speaking with scores of

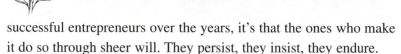

successful entrepreneurs over the years, it's that the ones who make it do so through sheer will. They persist, they insist, they endure.

So, too, can you.

So here's my final piece of advice: get started. There's only so much one can learn from books. It's the difference between reading travel guides and language books about a foreign country and then actually traveling there. One of my favorite scenes in my favorite movie, *A Hard Day's Night*, comes when Paul's mischievous grandfather berates Ringo for spending too much time with his "honker in a book." When Ringo replies "Books are good," Paul's grandfather snaps, "Paradin's better."

I guess one could say pretty much the same thing about starting a business. Books sure are good. But now it's time for you to start parading.

INDEX

ABOUT THE AUTHOR

Tom Ehrenfeld is a business journalist with more than a dozen years of experience in both print and radio. A former writer/editor at *Harvard Business Review* and *Inc.*, Ehrenfeld's work has also appeared in publications including the *New York Times* and *Boston Magazine*. He is a frequent speaker on small business issues and a regular commentator on PRI's Marketplace. To share more information on starting your company, please visit **www.startupgarden.com**.